MW00711123

With His Joy:

The Life and Leadership of David McKenna

by Donald E. Demaray

Light
& LIFE
COMMUNICATIONS

With His Joy:The Life and Leadership of David McKenna
BY DONALD E. DEMARAY

Illustrations and cover design
BY TAL BURDINE

ISBN: 0-89367-255-6

Scripture quotations are taken from the *New International Version* (NIV), *King James Version* (KJV), *New King James Version* (NKJV), *Revised Standard Version* (RSV) and *New Revised Standard Version* (NRSV).

© 2000 Light and Life Communications
Indianapolis, IN 46253-5002

Table of Contents

CREDITS

Dr. John VanValin, publisher for Light and Life Communications, conceived the idea of putting together a life of David L. McKenna. Without his creative initiative, the project would never have come to fulfillment. Thank you, John.

Faithful helpers throughout this endeavor included secretaries Tracy Hoffman, Laurie Verry and Melanie Fierbaugh. Donna Young, research assistant, never failed to provide answers to exploratory questions and to do specific assignments. Thank you to these four ladies.

Florence Mannoia remembered a most delightful story to fit perfectly into the final chapter of the book. Grace Yoder, Asbury Seminary archival worker—and a diligent one!—supplied help and materials. My loyal in-house editor, Kathleen, never fails to put my writing into perspective, clarifying both goals and information. Assistant editor Sheila Lovell, longtime secretary to Dr. McKenna, employed her considerable skills in making a better manuscript.

Thank you, editor Miriam Olver, Jeanne Acheson-Munos and others at Light and Life who took care of the final details of completing the book.

And thanks to the countless people who over the years filled my memory bank and put the color of laughter, feeling and reality into stories—really! I would get into trouble if I started to name persons, for surely I would leave out many.

Most especially I must thank David McKenna for patiently answering questions, making a flying trip to Wilmore, sharing in phone conversations and exchanging e-mails galore. Our friendship spans nearly half a century, and we never fail to connect, usually with a good story (he has more good ones than I).

D.D.

PREFACE

Three motifs mark the life of David L. McKenna. They express themselves at every turn in interviews, phone conversations, e-mails, published works, casual visiting. The three aspects strike us with heaven's beauty and define the fulfillment of his life. They also give us the purpose of this book: to describe and celebrate a life dedicated to Jesus Christ and His ministry.

God's will. The grand secret of abundant life, David believes, lies in doing God's will. Not *my* will, *His* will. You will read with interest and fascination about the struggle to say yes to His plan rather than David's dreams, because the inner battle is the fight of every human being exposed to the gospel. The yeses began in seminary, but they continued through five decades of active Christian ministry and go on to this day.

God's joy. The natural upshot of obedience is joy. Yes to God results in going with the grain of life, not against it. This explains Dave's laughter, storytelling and the signing of nearly every communiqué, "With His joy." Joy presents itself on every occasion, even in the dark valleys and difficult challenges. As you read, watch for the joy of the Lord which is strength.

God's grace. "Over and again in your writings and in your speeches and in conversation," I said to Dave, "grace appears. Why?" You should have heard the answer: it went on for some time, occasionally with tears. "I cannot believe it! A kid who grew up in a holiness Tabernacle, in a home with no real material benefits, a mom and dad uneducated and with almost no money—in other words, no advantages, and yet look!" I urged him to say more. "All the kids I grew up with in the legalistic Tabernacle eventually dropped out of the church; only my sister and I have stayed true to Christ."

Before I could say more, David went on: "My parents knew how to work. They worked hard. With them as models, I learned to put my shoulder to the wheel. But God gave me energy and drive and know-how. We had enough to eat and clothes for our backs. We never lived in poverty. Why? Grace."

"God graced my parents with the knowledge that my sister, Pat, and I needed a good education. We got it." This particular grace of God impresses Dave so much and so often, that over and again he mentions it: awe of the grace God provided for an extra good education. We'll talk more about this later.

And money? When that subject comes up, he has a lot to say. He began life with nothing. Literally. But God has blessed him, and he accounts for this on the basis of unmerited grace, and explains it in terms of John Wesley's stewardship principle: "Make all you can, save all you can, give all you can." David McKenna and his wife, Janet, have lived by that rule throughout a lifetime of service.

The context in which David operates is rich with the spirit of generosity. One of his role models, Dr. J. C. McPheeters, served as president of Asbury Theological Seminary while David was doing his ministerial studies. "Dr. Mac," as we called him, believed that when he visited someone, the first task related to ministry, not money. After retiring as president, Dr. McPheeters was a seminary fundraiser for many years. The Beeson money, one of the largest single donations to higher education in the history of American philanthropy, came as a result of years of ministry to the Beeson family. Spiritual ministry first, said Julian McPheeters. Giving follows.

Martin Luther declared that one's wallet defines the level of one's spirituality. The generous but careful steward of money knows God; after all, both the Christian and the money belong to God. People marked by generosity give not only their money, but their whole lives—time, talents, everything. Quietly, without wanting to attract attention, David has lived out Martin Luther's teaching on the wallet.

That context explains David and Janet McKenna's relationship to money. Salary? Secondary. A cut in pay if necessary? Not important in the light of God's will and grace. Investments? Do so moderately but regularly. Tithing? Always. Real estate? Well, presidents do not own their own houses, so why not put money to work as if one owned his own home? God's work? The church, publications to spread the gospel, scholarships at Christian colleges—all call loud and clear for attention. The McKennas strove to put ministry first, but giving always followed closely.

Today as he looks back, David sums up his passion for Christian ministry and responsible stewardship succinctly: " 'Make . . . save . . . give all you can' is a valid principle that I am not sure this generation hears and knows. With the coming transfer of wealth between generations, how I long for that message to be heard!" Obedience to God's will, living and working in the resultant joy of the Lord and watching with holy reverence God's grace at work in every dimension of life—well! that in summary tells the story of David McKenna. David's passion is to spread that threefold secret of fulfilled living.

Donald E. Demaray
Asbury Theological Seminary

For Janet

The loving and supportive
wife of David McKenna
Much loved mother and grandmother
Gracious friend to a host of admirers

AUTOBIOGRAPHICAL FOREWORD

Why doesn't David McKenna write his own autobiography? The answer is that I tried. In my mid-forties, I wrote down the story of my teenage years when I was under the heel of hellfire and brimstone preaching. At that time, however, I had to write the book as fiction in order to protect the characters who were still alive. Several titles came to mind. One was *Elmer Gantry Rides Again* because the preacher played a trombone, and another was *Peyton Place Revisited* because of all the sexual shenanigans that went on as a sideshow to the main event. I chose *Growing Up Holy*. At least this title reflected the positive as well as the negative aspects of a rigid holiness church.

But the more I wrote, the more I realized that I could not stay stuck in the past. While attending Wheaton Bible Church one day, I heard Chris Lyons preach on the upbringing of the prophet Samuel. Chris said, "One day it dawned on me. I was trying to protect my children from everything that led me to God." In a flash of insight, I knew that God had worked through the human strictures and religious foibles to keep me on the path toward His good will. From then on, all of the horror stories of growing up holy looked ludicrous and laughable rather than demeaning and debilitating. With a stroke of the pen, I changed the title to *Amusing Grace*. Yes, I did try to get it published under a pen name, but a memorable pink slip came back informing me that the book lacked the fictional quality of character development. Today, *Amusing Grace* is buried in the files waiting for some curious great-grandchild to read. It shall remain there.

Why did David McKenna permit a biography to be written? John Van Valin, publisher of Light and Life Communications, took me by surprise when he said that he wanted to do it. Of course, I was flattered. Only blue bloods in the faith and bishops of the church deserve a biography. I mildly demurred, but John persisted. Knowing me so well, he sweetened the request by saying that he would ask Donald Demaray to be the author. Nothing could please me more. Dr. Demaray is a dear friend and author of note who has the uncanny gift of getting inside the mind and soul of people, whether great saints or humble servants.

Still, I had a concern. Donald Demaray is also one of the gentlest and most gracious persons I have ever known. My fear was that he would canonize me because he sees, hears and speaks only good about people and circumstances. He is my model of a person who awakens every morning to commune with his Father and then carries the contagious spirit of Christ into every relationship of life. So, a caveat was struck. I would write this autobiographical foreword without knowing what Dr. Demaray had written about me in his book. Accordingly, I have chosen four autobiographical statements as a testimonial of the "inner man."

I am not a saint.

G. K. Chesterton defined a saint as "one who exaggerates what the world neglects." I do not qualify. I must confess that the world has been "too much with me" in my ambitions and achievements, and throughout my life I have run hot and cold on spiritual disciplines. More often than not, my career required an outlook that dealt with such mundane things as operating budgets and decisions that must be made when the buck stops in the office of the president. Even as a seminary president, I was perceived more as an executive-educator than as servant-pastor. Also, I remember the bruising lesson that I received from Kenneth Hansen, when he was jointly chairman of the board of Servicemaster and Wheaton College. With the frankness of a good mentor, Ken said, "Dave, you are so articulate that it took a long time before I could believe that you were real." That hurt because it showed the dark side of a gift behind which I protected myself.

I did, however, have one brush with sainthood during my career. After reading the book *Holy Company: Christian Heroes and Heroines*, by H. Elliott Wright, I was bolstered by

10

the evidence he presents that saints throughout the ages were human beings "hobbling toward holiness" with an "insatiable thirst for God." Suddenly, I felt myself part of that company, limping along the narrow way and panting after the heart of God. Come to think of it, I probably came closest to sainthood during my most worldly moment.

Dr. Demaray will undoubtedly tell the story of my appointment by Governor Dan Evans as chairman of his Blue Ribbon Committee to study gambling in the state of Washington. Because of my identity as a conservative Christian and president of Seattle Pacific College (later University), the local newspaper described the appointment as "asking the devil to guard the Holy Font." Savvy politicians warned me about the hazards of the position, which included the probability of bribes and the possibility of bombs. For the first time in my life, I could not count on my competency to carry my leadership. As a college president, for example, I could rely upon my credentials as one of the first persons to graduate from the University of Michigan with a Ph.D. in Higher Education Administration. But there is no academic preparation for chairing a gambling commission, and certainly, I had no experience in the field. Each day, then, I threw myself into God's arms and asked that He carry me. He did, but how soon we forget. As Henri Nouwen reminds us in his book on leadership titled *In the Name of Jesus,* the temptation to depend upon our competency is an occupational hazard that works against spirituality and any idea of sainthood.

My limping gait on the narrow road especially shows itself in my lifetime of spiritual struggles. Although I have an advanced degree in counseling psychology, I have no patience with people who blame their past for their present condition. If I did blame my past, I could tell a story of spiritual abuse that would top them all. How well I remember reading Jonathan Edwards's sermon "Sinners in the Hands of an Angry God" and identifying with his sinful listeners whose knuckles turned white as they gripped the pew in order to avoid falling into the flames of hell. No description of my spiritual heritage is more vividly accurate. I survived

11

those fears, but not without residual guilt that made me unsure of my salvation throughout the years.

Some might argue that it was the "perfectionism" as preached in the doctrine of holiness that kept me going to the altar week after week during my teenage years. Others might contend that my guilt reflected the weakness in Wesleyan theology that made "backsliding" an ever-present threat. For me, however, it was the nature of my sin that kept me from the assurance of full forgiveness. Early on, I learned the childhood lesson, "If you are gonna color the wall, do it behind the couch." The fear of hell drove my sins into secret places known only to God and me. My unending trips to the altar on Sunday night and during revival services surprised most of the church folk who saw me as different from the other teens who openly displayed their rebellion. Adding to my dilemma, the saintly women of the church anointed me as their "preacher boy."

If only they knew. Hanging around my neck was an albatross of guilt. When our junior high school literature class read Edward Arlington Robinson's poem "Richard Cory," presumably a model citizen until he put a pistol to his head, I felt inwardly, "That's me!" In high school, I heard for the first time Carlyle's response to the jeering crowd at a public hanging, "Except for the grace of God, there go I," and I thought, "That's me!" When my college reading introduced me to C. S. Lewis's autobiography *Surprised by Joy,* and I read how God revealed in him "a zoo of lust, a bedlam of hate, and a nursery for fears," again I said, "That's me!" Much, much later, during my middle-age years, David Seamands's book *Healing for Damaged Emotions* spoke to me about memorable quotes from our parents that could spiritually cripple us. I remembered Mom telling me time after time, "Be sure your sins will find you out." Once again, I said, "That's me!"

Secretly, I envied the Baptist kids who basked in the confidence of being "once saved, always saved." Intellectually, however, my Wesleyan roots went too deep. Calvinist theology simply didn't connect either with my experience or with the promptings of the Holy Spirit as I read the Word of God. Years went by before I discovered that I had been short-changed on my Wesleyan theology. John Wesley preached the doctrine of assurance as the counterpart to John Calvin's predestination. For me, it translated into the scriptural question that Wesley's converts heard weekly in their class meetings, "Does the Spirit witness with your spirit that you are a child of God?"

From then on, this question became my checkpoint when Satan tried to hang the burden of guilt around my neck. By asking this question, I opened myself to the scrutiny of the Spirit. If I sinned and the Spirit pointed it out, I immediately asked forgiveness through the blood of Christ and rested in the assurance of His love. Often, I liken myself to a member of Alcoholics Anonymous. At the beginning of the day, I ask God to keep me from sin and at the end of the day, I ask myself the Wesleyan question. The answer is either to confess a sin brought to mind by the check of the Holy Spirit or give thanks for an unblemished day in His will. It took a Calvinist friend, James I. Packer, who wrote, *Knowing God,* to teach me that holiness is a relationship with God as His child, not a regimen of expectations, which we can never meet. In that confidence, I go to sleep in peace and awaken humming one of my favorite hymns, written by Charles Wesley:

> Almighty God of truth and love,
> To me Thy power impart,
> The burden of my soul remove,
> The hardness of my heart.
> O may the least omission pain
> My reawakened soul,
> And drive me to the blood again,
> Which makes the wounded whole!

I am an example of God's grace.

If my life story began with a scriptural text, I would choose John 1:16: "And of His fullness we have all received, and grace for grace"(NKJV). The imagery behind this text is the unfathomable depths of an ocean of love with its waves of grace breaking incessantly on the shore. In every age and at every stage of my life, God's unmerited favor has washed over my soul.

Spiritually, I have experienced the grace of God leading me, saving me, and sanctifying me. Looking back, I see the traces of leading or prevenient grace keeping me from the deepest of sins, correcting my attempts to subvert His will, and preparing the way for changes in career. With the greatest of joy, I recall experiencing saving grace at the age of twelve and singing, "There's a new name written down in glory, and it's mine." Nor can I forget the peace of sanctifying grace that came to my soul at Asbury Theological Seminary when I surrendered my ambition to achieve a Ph.D. and accepted the call to go to India. How I wish that each of those moments could be engraved in stone. But no, they are only way stations on the road where grace intervenes time and time again. Perhaps this is why I am so impatient with static Christianity, fixed in place and dead in the water. For me, the Christian life is an adventurous pilgrimage, always moving forward toward brighter, broader, and better horizons.

Even though my spiritual experiences are "theologically correct" in Wesleyan terms, they only serve as background for the countless points of grace in my personal life. At the age of six months, my infant life hung in the balance through the night while my grandmother prayed. At the age of sixty-eight I flirted with death by playing through heart pains on the tennis court. Only grace can explain why I am alive today.

Only grace can explain why both my sister and I hold Ph.D.'s from the University of Michigan. Even though our father was a high-school dropout and our mother never went to high school, they believed in education for their children and sacrificed to put my sister and me through college. As a kid from holiness Tabernacle on the wrong side of tracks, I was a speckled bird in high school and a religious suspect in a Free Methodist college. Only grace can explain why I am coming to fifty years as a minister, educator and historian in the Free Methodist Church.

During my childhood years, my father and mother passed on religious convictions and moral values that held me through the trauma of their divorce and death. However, as a young adult, I was told that I was conceived before wedlock and became the reason for a loveless marriage. Only grace can explain why God gave me Janet, an itinerant pastor's daughter schooled in the public eye, as my loving wife and unexcelled First Lady of the presidential manse. An itinerant career has taken our family from Michigan to Kentucky, back to Michigan, on to Washington State, back to Kentucky, on to Nevada and finally back home to Seattle. Only grace can explain why Janet and I are celebrating our fiftieth wedding anniversary in 2000.

Thirty consecutive years as a college, university and seminary president take their toll on family life. Only grace can explain why our four children and their spouses are all alumni of the Christian university, leaders in their professions, faithful to their Lord and blessed by strong and loving families.

On the average, college presidents have a short tenure of four or five years, and few have the leverage of leadership to make significant changes in the institutions where they serve. Only grace can explain why I played a part in developing a four-year Christian liberal arts college, brought another Christian college to university status and saw a freestanding seminary receive the largest single gift in American history.

Most of all, the combination of physical, intellectual, emotional and spiritual fatigue in the high-stress job of leadership can grind away your vitality and darken your outlook in the later years of life. Only grace can explain why I awaken to every new day with anticipation, strike a note of joy with common people in ordinary settings and find myself humming another hymn of Charles Wesley from deep within my subconscious mind:

> O, to grace how great a debtor,
> Daily I'm constrained to be.
> Let thy grace, Lord, like a fetter,
> Bind my wandering soul to Thee.

Prone to wander, Lord, I feel it.
Prone to leave the Lord I love.
Take my heart, O, take and seal it.
Seal it for the courts above.

I have an insatiable thirst for God.

Returning to the book *Holy Company*, two common characteristics are described by the author as being shared by saints. One is their spiritual gait, which is described as "hobbling toward holiness"; the other is their "insatiable thirst for God." Once again, I am encouraged to know that even those whom we honor as saints did not feel as if they had "arrived" spiritually. They would be the first to deny the accolades of sainthood that the passage of time thrust upon them. I like them better as hobbling and thirsting like all of us. Another autobiographical reflection will tell you why.

My parents almost named me "Samuel." Dad, who drove the express Greyhound bus between Detroit and Chicago, had an African-American steward named Samuel who served the passengers on the route. They became such close friends that Dad wanted me to have his name. At the last minute, however, I suspect that Grandma McKenna prevailed, and I was christened "David—the beloved." In more than one sense, I wish that I were named Samuel. For one thing, my name would symbolize my father's love for a black man, long before the issue of equality became popular. For another thing, Samuel, the wise and upright judge of Israel, has always been my favorite.

In terms of my life story, however, I must confess that I identify more with David, whom Samuel anointed as the king of Israel. One reason is that the young David was known as a man after God's own heart. At the same time, his humanity kept him in trouble to the end of his days. He not only ruled with greatness and sang with sweetness, but also killed with despotic intention and sinned with devilish arrogance. Even in his final charge to Solomon on his deathbed, he was a bundle of contradictions, wavering between righteousness before God and retribution against his enemies.

How then can David be remembered as the greatest king of Israel from whose lineage the Messiah would come and whose psalms still bring us into the presence of God? The theological answer is easy. Even though David was a man after God's own heart, he represented the extremes of our humanity in his desire for God and his disobedience against God. Only the "Son of God" could be the man who lived without sin in the presence of God. The human reason is not so easy. I see myself in David. Knowing my own soul, I too am a bundle of contradictions, vacillating between spiritual highs and lows. At one and the same time, I thank God for the interventions of grace that have kept me from the extreme sin that we see in David, but I have also fallen short of his lofty psalms that sing God's praise. At best, I know the constancy of his thirst for God.

A picture comes to mind. While our son Rob and I were traveling together in the Holy Land, our guide led us from the desert plain up through scrubby brushland and along craggy paths. We stood by the cool, clear waters of a pool at the base of the cliffs of En-Gedi, where David hid in a cave to escape Saul. On the way to that sanctuary, as we followed the path along a trickling rivulet of water, our guide pointed out small deer that came to the water to drink. Spontaneously, he began to recite David's psalm, which might well have been written by the inspiration of the same scene:

"As the deer pants for streams of water,
so my soul pants for you, O God" (Psalms 42:1, NIV).

My soul resonated with his words and I knew why I identified with the man after whom I was named.

I have discovered the way of joy.

The grace note of joy has set the tone for my life, both personally and professionally. In the first year of my presidency at Seattle Pacific College, we called in consultants to help us create a realistic vision for the future. One of those persons was a Stanford scholar who specialized in consulting with private, liberal arts colleges. When he arrived on campus, he said to me, "Dave, you need to know that I am secular humanist. Your catalog says that you are an 'evangelical Christian' liberal arts college affiliated with the Free Methodist Church of North America. I don't know what that means, but I am going to find out." After spending a week on the campus, visiting with trustees, administrators, faculty, students and staff, he returned to my office for a summary session. He began by repeating, "You say that you are an 'evangelical Christian' liberal arts college affiliated with the Free Methodist Church of North America." Then he added, "I am still not quite sure what that means, but I do know this, if you are what you say you are, this campus will be characterized by a note of joy!"

It took an avowed secular humanist to show me the essence of our Christian faith. From then on, a "note of joy" became the tone and the theme of my personal and professional life. Eight years later, when a visiting team of examiners came from our regional accrediting agency, they reported, "We have never seen a campus where faculty, staff and students find so many reasons to celebrate." No higher commendation could be given to a Christian college.

Saint I am not, but I am an example of grace with an insatiable thirst for God and a joyous freedom as I trust in Christ. No one will wonder, then, why I claim Charles Wesley's hymn as my own song:

O, for a thousand tongues to sing,
My great Redeemer's praise.
The glories of my God and King;
The wonders of His grace.

With His Joy,
David L. McKenna
Seattle, Washington

John Wesley

Principle of Stewardship

"Make all you can,
Save all you can,
Give all you can."

Principle of Ministry

"Do all the good you can,
By all the means you can,
In all the ways you can,
In all the places you can,
At all the times you can,
To all the people you can,
As long as ever you can."

THE TRAVELER
A Spiritual Journey

Wrestling, I will not let thee go,
'Til I thy name, thy nature know.
—Charles Wesley (1707-1788)

THE TRAVELER:
A Spiritual Journey

C. S. Lewis, in *Pilgrim's Regress*, paints a bleak picture of spiritual travel. Some think the famous writer really speaks autobiographically; he certainly knew the arduous character of the road to Christlikeness, clearly documented in *Surprised by Joy*, his official autobiography. In Book Six of the *Regress*, Lewis pictured three hikers. They hated the landscape—boring, flat, and uninteresting—only a scrub bush here and a bit of grass there. The brown earth, mixed with rock and moss, coupled with unbroken cloud cover, made the journey very tedious. Birds were not even singing. And when the travelers stopped to rest, sweat turned instantly cold on their bodies. The trio plodded on many miles until the sky turned "from sunless gray to starless black." Finally, they spotted a shanty along the roadside where they paused in their travel.

For David McKenna, the journey began on a cloudy day in Michigan.

"Just a Tabernacle Kid"

Sensing my awareness of his struggles and the overcoming grace of God in his life, he concluded one of our frequent e-mail messages, "Remember, I am just a Tabernacle kid." Therein begins a story, unlike Lewis's landscape, anything but tedious, though often cloudy, and like Lewis's story, rugged and rocky.

More than seven decades ago now, a Greyhound bus driver met a beautiful, warm cabaret dancer. Patrons gladly paid a hard-earned dime for each dance with her. Known as a taxi dancer, she met the handsome bus driver in Detroit, though she came from Fitchburg, Massachusetts. She envisioned herself someday as a Ziegfeld Follies performer and aimed to invest her life in the glamorous entertainment world. Instead, her relationship with the bus driver resulted in pregnancy and then marriage. The baby's name? David. The family moved to Sturgis, Michigan, which was convenient for Dad because the town was a stop on his route from Detroit to Chicago.

Dad's bus had its own rest room and dining area, with a steward named Samuel. Before the baby's birth on May 5, 1929, Mom and Dad debated over a name: Samuel or David? Clearly, the bus driver and the steward were close friends.

The joy that came with the baby's birth did not last long, for the six-month-old contracted a most serious disease; the medical people called it erysipelas. Few infants survived the critical illness. A blood clot formed in his right arm, then moved to his back, and a single night would tell whether the little fellow would live or die because the clot might move to the heart and kill him.

David's concerned mom called her mother, a grandmother who knew how to pray. She stayed on her knees all night. Victory came with the first rays of sun, and years later Grandma told David of God's clear message that came to her on that decisive night: "I received the promise of your healing, and gave you to God for a life of Christian service." Years later he recalled the story of John Wesley's rescue from the burning parsonage. Wesley called himself a "brand plucked from the burning." "Perhaps God also had something for me to do," reasoned David McKenna.

Tiny David's return to health led to the conversion of both his mother and father. Now Grandpa and Grandma McKenna, along with the young parents, joined a holiness church known as the Evangelical Missionary Tabernacle. Located in Ypsilanti, Michigan, the Tabernacle related to a movement that had started in Adrian, Michigan, in rebellion against the "liberal" Free Methodist denomination. These fundamentalists had broken with the mother denomination in the 1920s. The term "radical" defined them. Plain dress, no makeup, no jewelry—and many more negatives—set them apart from the rest of the world. Indeed, the emphasis on negatives segregated them from most of the church universal because they believed the "popular" churches supported the works of the devil. Legalism marked the Tabernacle people.

The antics of preachers and people, the shouting and the "exhortations," the sermons and testimonies centered in un-controlled expressions and legalistic concerns. The music and the preaching, often uncultivated and crude, exposed the general lack of education of these simple people.

Conversion to Christ

Yet in spite of the shortcomings of this setting, God's Word bore fruit. David's grandfather came to Christ, as did many others, and David got his real introduction to the gospel in Bill O'Neal's Sunday School class, made up of five- and six-year-old boys. Bill had no teaching skills—the class never did come under control—but the teacher had won the state swimming championship and provided a role model for the young lads. "If a swim champ can be a Christian," reasoned young David, "I can be a Christian, too." Eventually Bill married David's aunt and so became Uncle Bill and a lifelong mentor.

Dan Baughey, the preacher at the Tabernacle, played the trombone, and from him David got his inspiration to learn the instrument. The pastor swayed and strutted about the platform as he led congregational singing, and David saw himself someday capturing the limelight in the same way.

At the tender age of eight, David heard a sermon about twelve-year-old Jesus talking with the wise old teachers in the Temple. The preacher announced his subject as "The Age of Accountability" and defined it, of course, as age twelve. Relief for young David! He had four more years to "live it up," to sin to his heart's content. He could swim with the fellows and have a cigarette; he could skip school to see a movie; he could tell the occasional lie to protect himself. He could live free, for had not the preacher said that one did not have to live responsibly—for his sins, at least—until age twelve? "I can wait to get saved until later," he said to himself. And yes, when he reached twelve he did indeed accept the Way of Salvation. But he had problems with "the Way": that is, with the Tabernacle's definition of the Way. Testimonies to personal salvation, for example.

The night came when David's aunt demanded that the kids in the youth group testify to the New Birth. She assigned testimonies alphabetically by last names. The sequence began. The A's witnessed, then the B's and the C's until all had spoken through the L's. No doubt to encourage young David, Mom, Dad, Grandpa and Grandma McKenna all spoke. Even seven-year-old sister could say a good word for the Lord. But David? A long wait. Every eye focused on the lad. In the awful silence, the boy finally stood to his feet, though he must have surprised even himself when he announced, "I don't have a testimony. Pray for me."

The drama that now took place, painted for all time on heaven's canvas, would mark the beginning of a long and colorful spiritual journey. All in the room fell to their knees. David made a beeline for the sawhorse altar in the front of the church. Everyone prayed aloud. Despite the noise and confusion, David made authentic confession of his sins and entered the Kingdom. He now stood, ready to give testimony to forgiveness and God's grace. "I don't recall what I said," remembered David, "but I will never forget riding home in the old, gray, 1938 Plymouth. As we crossed the bridge over the river, my father broke into song, 'There's a new name written down in glory . . . .' For the first time I could sing the refrain, 'And it's mine, O yes it's mine.'"

Only two years later, he sensed God's invitation into

Christian ministry. He had thought of the engineering profession, but now the call came as he read Romans 10:15: "How beautiful are the feet of them that preach the gospel of peace, and bring glad tidings of good things" (KJV). David McKenna had begun what would eventuate in a most re-markable Kingdom career.

Ugly Duckling Days

In high school David's lifestyle clashed with that of his fellow students. A regular guy he was not. He could not drink with the fellows, or have a smoke; he could not take a date to a school dance; he could not even attend the movie theater. And playing poker? Out!

The holiness Tabernacle regulated the lives of the youth with the stringency of the Pharisees. Six services a week helped keep the kids out of trouble. Add to that the revivals that took place every three months, each revival ex-tending over a two-week period! Moreover, on Saturday nights all had to go to the street meetings for public wit-ness. At all services, everyone had to show up and listen to the hellfire sermons. Preaching at the Tabernacle always ended with long calls to come forward for prayer at the sawhorse altar. The oldsters cried aloud, pleading with the boys huddled together on the back rows of the Tabernacle to stop their sinning.

David McKenna wrote an autobiographical novel, *Amusing Grace,* which was never published but expresses the conflicts of those Tabernacle years. One of the stories from this work of autobiographical fiction suggests the na-ture of the worship services. David took trombone lessons; yes, he wanted to perform on the platform like his Taber-nacle pastor, leading congregational singing with the wave of the trombone slide, marching down the aisle, becoming a "leader."

In real life David learned to play the trombone well. In

fact, he made first chair in marching band by his junior year in high school. But how would he play in the band and go to Friday night revival meeting at the Tabernacle? He devised a way. Appearing at church in uniform, he left the service at nine o'clock sharp, running to his high school football field in the nick of time to take lead place in the marching band's half-time performance.

Tennis, too, came in for its ridicule. Dave, captain of his high school tennis team, appeared for a photograph, not in the white shorts everyone else wore, but in long pants. There he stood with his teammates, in front of the net, different from the others! Tabernacle legalism pronounced shorts sinful. But on the sly, David played in tennis shorts. A girl in his church reported on him to the pastor; whereupon the minister preached against such behavior! In David's presence, of course.

David felt like the ugly duckling. The mother duck sat on her eggs, goes the old story, but one egg appeared strange. A patriarchal duck talked to the mother, announcing that the odd egg would mean disappointment. "Ignore it," he commanded. But mother ducks do not turn their backs on duty. She continued to sit on the eggs, and one day they hatched— that is, all but the one big, curious egg. The unusual egg eventually brought new life, but not the usual duckling. The chicks avoided the curiosity, yet the mother sensed that the strange creature would turn into something grand. She had brought to life a swan. Now the bird would have to develop into its intended destiny.

College Days

David's mom and dad, dropouts from high school, felt comfortable in the holiness Tabernacle where most did not get a complete education. Nor did Dave's high school mates go through college. Yet David's parents possessed sufficient insight to know that their son should go on to further schooling.

Dad and Mom took him to visit college campuses, though his Tabernacle people tried to insist he attend God's Bible School in Cincinnati, Ohio. Coming home from their tour of that school, the family stopped in Coldwater, Michigan at a grocery store. Inside they noticed a flyer announcing a revival at the local Free Methodist church. To make a long story short, through the Coldwater church the McKennas discovered Spring Arbor College, where David attended, graduating in 1949 with an associate of arts degree, and eventually becoming president of the institution. The providence of that whole scenario prompts David McKenna to recall Robert Frost's "The Road Not Taken," the last three lines of which read

> Two roads diverged in a wood, and I—
> I took the one less traveled by,
> And that has made all the difference.

The Tabernacle people called Spring Arbor "that liberal college" because it represented the Free Methodism from which they had fled in protest. Only Bible schools knew the Word of God. Nor did dress at the college suit the holiness people back home where young ladies wore their hair in plain style, donned gingham dresses and put on what Dave called "orthopedic shoes."

Once at Spring Arbor in the fall of 1947, however, he felt a new freedom. He noticed a pretty girl, with a gleam in her eye, who lighted his world. In fact, she seemed to light up everyone's world as she walked about campus and attended class. What puzzled David at first related to her appearance: bobbed hair, bobby socks, even a bit of lipstick. Could she know God like the young ladies back home? Finally, Dave loosened his grip on the rigid style of his home church and began to find the liberty of the sons and daughters of the Resurrection. That pretty girl, Janet Ruth by name, turned out to be the daughter of the college pastor! That too helped relieve David of his overly strict conditioning.

David Loren McKenna and Janet Ruth Voorheis married on June 9, 1950, and at age 19, David took her with him into a pastorate. But he was a kid from the Evangelistic Mission Tabernacle, and the clergy of the Free Methodist conference opposed his acceptance into the Southern Michigan jurisdiction. E. A. Cutler, the conference superintendent, stood up for the candidate: "I don't know if you will accept this young man, but I will appoint him to a church." That this fledgling minister had just married the daughter of one of the best-loved pastors in the conference did not hurt David's chances either!

So the bride and groom went to Vicksburg, Michigan. But such a church! The former pastor, who had just been dismissed, did not reflect the situation in a very bright light. Even so, great things happened. The church appointment supported David while he continued his college training at Western Michigan University. He did, in fact, take a full load and in June 1951 graduated *magna cum laude,* second in his class, with a major in history and a minor in psychology.

A delightful part of the church story relates to Janet. She had been a cheerleader at Spring Arbor, but now became—all at once!—"Sister McKenna," and also, automatically, head of the Women's Missionary Society. Those big changes came in just the first three months of their pastorate.

David preached with enthusiasm, the young couple sang, and they called on thirty elderly members. But their focus centered on the promising young people. The fruit of that focus resulted in the development of a strong youth department. They saw several soundly saved, some who still to this day contribute to the life, work and witness of the church.

David and Janet renovated the old church building, a dark and dirty place. They painted, papered, cleaned and made it so fresh and delightful that none other than the bishop himself, Charles V. Fairbairn, accepted an invitation to come and preach a rededication sermon. Janet found herself terribly nervous entertaining the bishop, so she called her mom to come help her.

After only a year at Vicksburg, the church enjoyed a growing place in both the Kingdom and the community, had a vital youth group and many new converts. To cap it all, David received ordination in the Southern Michigan Conference in 1952.

Surrender to God

Having finished college, David followed his call into Christian ministry by enrolling at Asbury Theological Seminary. He entered seminary intending to go into full-time pastoral work. But during his senior year, he sensed a different kind of call, namely, a call to Christian higher education. Now he aimed to go on to university and earn a Ph.D.

Professors had often asked David to substitute for them by lecturing in seminary classrooms. His quick, keen mind fascinated fellow students. Clearly he would experience no difficulty finding universities to welcome him into their doctoral programs. He even discovered places to work on the side while doing doctoral studies so he could support his little family, for now the babies began to come.

But God needed to deal with his self-centeredness. The Lord spoke through a veteran missionary to India, J. T. Seamands, who addressed seminary chapel one day during David's senior year. So vividly did J. T. describe the needs of India that David found himself wrestling with a call to that far-off land. "Surely, Lord, you do not mean me. I'm headed for a Ph.D." But God's voice would not stop. Finally, David skipped classes, went to his seminary apartment, and stayed on his knees until peace entered his soul. About 3 P.M. the battle came to a head; now he could pray, "Not my will but yours: India if You will; Ph.D. if You will. But *your* will." That prayer summarized his new surrender, and it became the motif of every career decision of his life.

"From that moment on, as best I know, His will has been the controlling center for my life decisions," he announces freely and publicly.

David never went to India; he did earn the Ph.D. With the David of Scripture he confesses, "I delight to do Thy will, O Lord."

God's Will: Moving Forward

Opportunities and possibilities along the way always met the test of God's will. David confesses, however, that he could have taken his life into his own hands and missed the Sovereign's plan. "Only my commitment to do God's will has kept me moving forward," he says forthrightly. But he had big dreams for himself, aspirations which God, in His providence, denied.

David McKenna dreamed of a seat in the United States Senate; of editing the prestigious evangelical journal *Christianity Today;* of serving as secretary of education under President Reagan; of sitting in the president's seat at the University of Washington. God declared a resounding no to each aspiration.

Yet, the dreamer in McKenna confesses, "Even now, I feel the tug of past ambition when I recall the list of positions which I have been denied." He aimed at a political career in his thirties, but a political leader in Michigan, where David then served as president of Spring Arbor College, offered counsel he did not fully expect. "You can influence more people as a college president than as a United States senator." Moreover, his friend asked David if he had the patience required to do politics. In the end, David decided he did not like what he heard.

In David's forties, he might have become editor of *Christianity Today,* but Billy Graham, the journal's founder and a board member, spoke to David in unrestrained language: "We thought about making you editor, but decided that we shouldn't take you away from the presidency of Seattle Pacific University." David's heart sank; he had really wanted the job and wished the magazine's board had talked to him before electing another man to give leadership to the magazine.

David had turned fifty years of age when Senator Mark Hatfield called early one morning, informing him of possible appointment as secretary of education in President Ronald Reagan's new administration. Time passed while the authorities looked for a woman or an ethnic to fill the position. David wanted to "run" for the position, making speeches, writing, doing whatever he could to win it. But Hatfield, who firmly believed in the sovereignty of God, refused to let David McKenna put himself forward. "If God is in it, it will be," declared the senator. Meanwhile, the president's office at Seattle Pacific had to cope with a flood of mail, plus calls from the media. All this did not make Hatfield's counsel easy. Washington, D.C., New York, and of course David's own city, Seattle, kept calling his Seattle Pacific office. Yet he could not "run" to get the position in Washington, D.C.

Actually, the McKennas did expect the appointment from President Reagan. It never came. On the morning of the Reagan announcement, television news carried the surprising information that Terry Bell would be secretary of education. Bell, not even a finalist, got the position, and in a curious sort of way. The Marriott Hotel's Bill Marriott, Reagan's biggest financial contributor, called the president to say, "We didn't get our man in commerce or labor. We want our man in education." A key stipulation was that the man must be a Mormon.

David felt very hurt by the Bell appointment. When television news showed Bell in a cabinet meeting in the Oval Office, David would say to himself, "That man's sitting in my seat." But repeatedly God spoke to him: "What if that Washington position had meant losing your family?" He had prayed that God's will would prevail. It had, yet the ambitious university president wrestled, and the inner battle went on for weeks.

Finally, while jogging along the beaches of Puget Sound, David heard Jeremiah's words loudly and clearly: "For surely I know the plans I have for you, says the Lord, plans for your welfare and not for harm, to give you a future with hope" (Jeremiah 29:11, NRSV). Resigning himself to God's plan, McKenna brought closure to the issue by announcing to his university community, "I'd rather be your president than Reagan's secretary." Now he knew, and students, faculty and staff all knew that Dr. McKenna meant business about doing God's will and God's will only.

Yet there was one further struggle with ambition. The presidency of the University of Washington opened, and some of Seattle's movers and shakers approached McKenna about this position. He reasoned, "I have challenged audiences and individuals who name the name of Christ to stand up and be counted in the public square. I must practice what I preach. In a public university presidential position, I could exercise my Christian principles." So went the thoughts in his head. He confessed openly, ". . . I felt as if this would be an opportunity to enter the 'crucible' of public higher education and make a difference as a Christian."

Surprise again, however. The university board did not take his name seriously. "In fact, I went out on the first cut because of my identity in Seattle as an educator in the wrong neighborhood. My witness as a Christian and my identity as a clergyman made me untouchable."

Also while serving as president of Seattle Pacific University, some Washington state leaders suggested he run for governor. The news got around. With his public speaking gifts, ability to solve knotty problems, endless energy—well, for all the world, people said, he could serve well as their head of state. But this too came to a cul-de-sac. Clearly, God would not let him travel any road but His.

The Asbury Seminary Story

The Asbury Theological Seminary Board invited David McKenna to interview for the presidency of the institution upon the retirement of Frank Bateman Stanger. Dr. Stanger had served well, putting up beautiful Georgian buildings, enhancing the faculty with fine scholars, working toward top-of-the-line scholarly respectability in both the Methodist and the larger seminary and theological communities. Stanger had indeed made a name for Asbury Theological Seminary, now a first-rate graduate school with multiple degree programs. No wonder the seminary board wanted an up-and-coming president to lead its theological community of students, faculty, staff and constituency. But when McKenna finished the board interview, he said no to the invitation, commenting that he could exercise influence in a wider sphere if he stayed with the Seattle Pacific University job.

Then the surprise came! (God's middle name is Surprise.) David went to speak at a conference of United Methodist higher education personnel. While he was there, an alumnus of Asbury Seminary said to David, "If you should ever go to Asbury, I and others would support you." What followed is best told in David's own words.

"Janet and I went to our room and wondered aloud, 'Did we say "no" too quickly?' Then and there, we agreed that we would do nothing, but if the call came back, we would have to give it consideration. In the fall, while I was watching Michigan play Notre Dame, Ira Gallaway, chairman of the board of trustees, called me and said, 'Nothing else seems right. Will you reconsider your decision?' Then, before I could answer him, another phone call came from a trustee. James Earl Massey called and in his inimitable way asked me, 'Is it possible that the Spirit is nudging you toward Asbury?' I accused him of being in collusion with Ira Gallaway. But he said, 'No, I've only been talking to God.' Within a month, I knew what God meant when He met me in my disappointment and informed me of His plans for me, plans for good, plans with a future and a hope."

And mixed up in all this, his denomination nearly elected him a bishop. His ascent to the episcopacy almost happened.

Many friends have asked, "What if David McKenna had become bishop instead of president of Asbury Theological Seminary?" Surely the Free Methodist Church of North America would have become more visible worldwide. Visibility, one of McKenna's aims wherever he does Kingdom work, would have come to a new reality for the denomination. Without question, Spring Arbor College, Seattle Pacific University and Asbury Theological Seminary became far better known as a result of his administration. Today Asbury Theological Seminary enjoys a place of status unparalleled in its history, known the world over, sending its graduates everywhere as pastors, missionaries, chaplains, counselors and executives.

A Big Decision on the Journey

The Christian College Consortium invited McKenna to become their president. This invitation came after he had served Asbury Theological Seminary for a decade. Actually the opportunity appealed to him. He could write his own ticket, work on the integration of faith and learning—the stated purpose of the Consortium—and see a career dream come true.

That dream had begun two decades earlier when McKenna conceived the idea of the Christian College Consortium. He had put together the proposal, applied for and received funding from the Lilly Endowment, and served as chairman of a consortium conference held at Indiana University. Now he had the chance of making strong a viable evangelical higher education thrust in the American community. "Here," he said, "was the opportunity to do research, writing, speaking and consulting as the next chapter in my spiritual journey. I heard the call and I wanted to say yes."

Just days after the Consortium invitation, President McKenna got word that at last, after many years, the Ralph Waldo Beeson will would now become financial reality. "I told the Consortium board that I would do nothing to jeopardize the Beeson will for Asbury." McKenna elaborated with this commentary: "Because I have changed presidencies three times, I entertained no pretense about my indispensability. Yet, because the will was revocable and Mr. Beeson had already revised it seven times, I knew our donor might think, 'If McKenna doesn't stick with it, why should I?'"

This dynamic led McKenna to announce to the Consortium board that he must delay any decision until the bequest proved fixed, genuinely secure. Mr. Beeson might die, leaving the will intact. He had reached his ninetieth birthday! So the Consortium board waited. Mr. Beeson passed away on October 15, 1991. The will now irrevocable, David expected release to take the Christian College Consortium position.

But release did not come. Instead, with the Divine "no" came peace that David did not need to look for another position. He must stay at Asbury. His testimony came to expression in five forthright sentences: "If Asbury is the last chapter, I will know no greater joy. In fact, I have never been so busy, so happy, so stretched and so scared as I am now. My spiritual journey has brought me to a new maturity in His will. I have been responsive to His call, and now I know the joy of being faithful to His task. I am set free to stay put."

Stay put he did while the $39 million bequest grew, buildings went up, and new programs took shape. Especially notable among the programs was the Beeson Pastors' Program. Dozens of promising ministers have become part of the program, enhancing their preaching skills, and further developing leadership gifts. The first program director, Wade Paschal, laid the foundation well. When he moved on to pastor a church, Bill Beachy took charge of overseeing the construction of the Beeson buildings. Bill later went into the pastorate, and today Dale Galloway serves as dean of the Beeson Center.

The Beeson program came into being because of the multimillion-dollar will and the intensive and focused efforts of David McKenna and Bill Conger, executor of the will. Early on, the two sat talking together one day when suddenly Conger declared, "I don't believe what's about to happen on this campus. To think it all started with a telephone call!" They agreed that God had invaded Asbury Seminary with enormous opportunity, and that He himself stood in charge of the whole affair. David's task, and Bill's too, was simply to let God do His thing, and to be faithful to whatever He assigned.

The upshot? A magnificent quad campus, enriched faculty, enhanced curriculum and enormous interest worldwide in Asbury Theological Seminary. Calls come from interested prospective students from all over the world. Even bus tours of central Kentucky stop to let customers see the beautiful campus and hear about what some call "the world's leading theological school in the Wesleyan tradition."

Retirement

David McKenna delivered thirty-three consecutive convocation addresses as president of Spring Arbor College, Seattle Pacific University and Asbury Theological Seminary. His last address, "Gifts of Succession," began with humor:

> "I have begun to collect jokes apropos to this year of succession which will lead to retirement. My favorite is the story of the undertaker who made the mistake of mixing up the favorite suits that two widows had chosen for their deceased husbands to wear at their funerals. Both services were scheduled at the same time, and the error was discovered too late to

make the change of clothes. To calm the widows, who insisted that their husbands be buried in their favorite suits, the creative undertaker assured them, 'No problem, *we'll just change heads!'"*

Change heads the seminary did. And David paved the way for the coming of the new president, Maxie Dunnam, in a gracious way. President McKenna did not let his ego get in the way, refusing to leave as a king or to create the impression that no one could possibly succeed him with sufficient gifts and graces to match his administration. He did not want the board to name him chancellor, nor did he wish to take an influential position in the management of the seminary. In fact, the McKennas moved out of town, building a house in Nevada and living near his sister, who needed support in her illness.

In his final convocation address at Asbury Theological Seminary, David quoted a litany by Leonard Sweet:

The world is a better place because Michelangelo didn't say, "I don't do ceilings."

The world is a better place because a German monk named Martin Luther didn't say, "I don't do doors."

The world is a better place because an Oxford don named John Wesley didn't say, "I don't do fields."

The world is a better place because Moses didn't say, "I don't do rivers."

The world is a better place because Noah didn't say, "I don't do arks."

The world is a better place because Jeremiah didn't say, "I don't do weeping."

The world is a better place because Amos didn't say, "I don't do speeches."

The world is a better place because Rahab didn't say, "I don't do carpets."

The world is a better place because Ruth didn't say, "I don't do mothers-in-law."

The world is a better place because David didn't say, "I don't do giants."

The world is a better place because Peter didn't say, "I don't do Gentiles."

The world is a better place because Mary didn't say, "I don't do virgin births."

The world is a better place because Mary Magdalene didn't say, "I don't do feet."

The world is a better place because John didn't say, "I don't do deserts."

The world is a better place because Paul didn't say, "I don't do letters."

The world is a better place because Jesus didn't say, "I don't do crosses."

Leonard Sweet missed one: The world is a better place because David McKenna didn't say, "I don't do the will of God."

The Secret

Toward the end of C. S. Lewis's *The Pilgrim's Regress,* he puts these words in the mouth of the pilgrim, "I heard the voice of the Guide. . . ." Just there lies the secret of doing the will of God.

THE CHALLENGER
A Life of Risk and Adventure

That I may justly say . . .
"I came, saw, and overcame."
—William Shakespeare
Cymbeline: Act 3, Scene 1

THE CHALLENGER:
A Life of Risk and Adventure

From "when I was quite a young child," reflected Robinson Crusoe, "I had felt a great wish to spend my life at sea." Through the early growing-up years, his taste for the sea grew "more and more strong." At last he broke loose from his home in York, England, went to Hull, and took a job on board a ship. But a frightful squall arose; on the fifth night, the vessel sprang a leak. The captain and crew lost their ship.

"Young lad," the lost ship's owner warned once they reached land, "you ought to go to sea no more, it is not the kind of life for you."

"Why, sir," Robinson replied, "will you go to sea no more then?"

"That is not the same kind of thing. I was bred to the sea, but you were not."

Nonetheless, the lad determined to return to the briny deep, finding employment on another ship that also had a disastrous end. Robinson landed on an island where he lived some twenty years, seldom seeing another human being except for his helper, Friday.

The plot of the famous *Robinson Crusoe* novel by Daniel Defoe centers in a succession of crises, each a formidable challenge, each threatening even to his life, but each issuing in victory and helping people escape tragedy to live a good life. The same has been true in David McKenna's life.

Relishing the Challenges

"I love the feel of the wind in my face," says David McKenna. He once wrote me an e-mail just before driving to

Lake Chelan where he moors his sailboat to say, "I can hardly wait to face the wind." Sailing has become a metaphor for meeting the challenges of life. "Taking advantage of the winds teaches me how to cope with life's winds of change."

"All our adventures were by the fire-side," writes Oliver Goldsmith in *The Vicar of Wakefield*. Not so with David McKenna. Reading and talking about adventure and risk may be one thing, but facing up to life's challenges is where David lives.

On one unusually snowy day in Seattle when the university was closed due to a storm both unexpected and unusual, David debated about going to the office. Finally he donned his suit and tie, left the president's residence on the hill, and ventured on foot, only to hear the excited call of the students: "Come, Prexy, ride down the hill on the sled!" Should he really? Wanting to be a good sport, he boarded the vehicle only to discover the pilot was cross-eyed! Landing at last, safe and sound at the bottom of the hill, David could only reflect on the harrowing experience with a laugh.

David McKenna relishes adventure and risk.

The Sport of It All

David McKenna played ice hockey as a kid, but had so little money to buy equipment that he had to create his own pucks. In addition, from his youth, David has played tennis. Making captain of his high school team, he developed a lifelong taste for the game. He loves playing, and at Spring Arbor College, Seattle Pacific University, and Asbury Theological Seminary, he challenged students and staff on the courts.

At Asbury, students announced an annual tennis tournament. David entered, winning game after game against students. Office staff got into the tournament; he invited them to close shop and come watch the semifinal match. It turned out to be an exciting game with David fielding shots meticulously, and winning! The final match he lost after dark, and D. Wray Richardson, longtime friend of the seminary and former staff member, came off with the winning cup.

Some Wins, Some Losses

Athletic events prime David for facing formidable puzzles and problems. The competition challenges his best. Formation of character and mindset for coming to grips with the ventures of life and presidential administration—these sum up the professional benefits he realizes from participating in competitive sports. A godly, bold self-confidence kept David McKenna's perspective intact through the hard and sometimes blistering provocations of his work. A maintenance man gets peeved with the president and resigns. An administrator disagrees with McKenna's fiscal philosophy and administrative policy; he too leaves his job. An academic dean threatens to vacate his post and then actually does so, talking out his complaints in frankness to the president.

David McKenna knows these kinds of events happen in the life of an institution. He refuses to allow atmospheres to develop that breed fierce argument, and always attempts to redeem losses. Instead, he sees conflict management as one of his chief tasks, and frequently puts people who have opted out of their jobs into other positions, hopefully more fitted to their gifts and graces.

He hurts and hurts deeply when criticized but resolutely refuses to focus on his wounds. Instead, he aims always to serve and, characterized by the holiness he believes and tries under God to practice, frequently sees enemies become friends. He takes on a Lincolnesque style, knowing that when he opens himself to learn from his critics and love them, he may indeed make them his friends, adding to both their character and his.

A Painful Battle

A different kind of challenge for David has been a life-long battle against feelings of spiritual inadequacy. The Tabernacle may have intensified this because of the hellfire sermons and legalism of early influences. "Have I really lived up to the gospel standard?" he asks himself. Earlier in life, he suffered from a morbid fear of losing his soul. And as a young person, week after week, he sought God at the Tabernacle sawhorse altar, never quite able to secure assurance of full salvation.

Fortunately, he did not become one of the spiritual rebels of his age group. He did commit what he remembers as "stealthlike" sins, done silently, secretly, taking cover from public radar. Consequently, if someone had inquired about his salvation, even long into his adulthood, he would not have answered with certainty. Guilt plagued him even after specific confession of sins. No wonder he longed, for a period, to become a Calvinist, just to know his salvation was secure.

Not until David began to explore Wesleyan theology in depth did he discover the teaching about assurance. One day he discovered the promise that the Spirit witnesses with one's own spirit, firmly establishing in the inner man adoption by God the Father (Romans 8:15-16). He sees the legalistic expression of Christianity heard in his youth as neglecting this New Testament doctrine of assurance.

Yet, even now, he confesses, he must check himself. Evil knows his point of vulnerability. In recent times, David McKenna has reread Chaucer's *Canterbury Tales*, and he sees there the dilemma of travelers who live with both a public image and a private persona. That fact of our humanity may not reveal hypocrisy, but it does point out the dilemma of human nature.

Secular psychotherapists, such as Freudians, might blame David's background for his struggle, but he has moved past all that and gets comfort in reading the lives of the saints, finding in every one of them their own peculiar spiritual struggles. That, he declares with genuine humbleness, keeps him from gloating over success or attempting to control people and situations. Yet he still feels unworthy, and knows within himself only that God has graced him with an insatiable desire for His Presence.

Souls in anguish have a special place in God's family.

The Whisper of His Grace

From the late 1970s to early 1990s, David entered into long-term study of several books of the Bible. Under the direction of the *Communicator's Commentary* series editor Lloyd Olgivie, David wrote the volumes on Mark, Job and Isaiah (published by Word Books, Texas). Usually works like these each took about a year, but the volume on Job took two.

Wrestling with the sufferings of Job yielded spin-offs in writing, speaking (he did a series on Job in the Asbury Seminary chapel), and publications such as *The Whisper of His Grace*. What strikes one about that book is the incisiveness of his questions, the utter realism of his perspective, and the biblical answers to the numbing question about evil in a world God rules. Such a realistic perspective can only come from personal suffering. An estranged father, a grandson who briefly ran away from home, a brother-in-law who died before his time, the loss of his mother, cataracts and eye surgery, arthritis, bypass surgery—like Robinson Crusoe, David McKenna has met crisis upon crisis.

Critical challenges paint themselves on mind and heart with big impact; grace whispers. The secret of victory? Listening to the divine whisper.

Eye Surgery

Even before Dr. McKenna took office at Asbury Theological Seminary, he suffered from eye problems, specifically cataracts. After assuming office, he struggled with reading while in pain. One morning his eyes played tricks on him and thinking he saw the breakfast table as usual, he missed it completely, breaking the coffeepot and spilling the coffee. Finally, he had to have surgery. Home from the hospital, he felt wave after wave of illness break over him. It was as if the ocean had engulfed him. Sympathetic friends and family called, ringing the phone off the hook. Finally, he had to shut off the telephone to get required rest and make possible the needed restoration so he could resume his presidential duties.

The surgery was less than perfect, and resulted in still further treatment. Days and weeks of discomfort came and went, and at last the eyes returned to normal. I asked him about his reading during the difficult days. "Oh," he said with dismay, "reading is my life. Few crises could hit me harder." However, the public never saw a complaining spirit.

The Story of a Heart

David's genes told him of his candidacy for heart disease. His grandfather had died of heart failure, and his father became its victim at age sixty-nine. His dad had suffered a massive heart attack; the paramedics revived him but not quickly enough to save him from the loss of oxygen—his brain had no oxygen for some thirteen minutes. The human brain can normally tolerate no more than four or five minutes without oxygen, and with the brain stem dead, Dad McKenna turned completely unresponsive.

David took seriously his genetic heritage, but thought he had won by a careful lifestyle: walking, running, tennis, racquetball—all became part of his regularized discipline. To this regimen he added dietary care. Running cleared his mind and brought solutions to difficult administrative problems as he jogged. Already possessed of a habitually positive attitude, "runner's high" solutions only enhanced his wholesome mental attitude. Over time, David developed not only a "runner's heart," but a "runner's mind." Good news for anyone threatened by any disease, much less something so serious as cardiac challenges.

But surprising and ominous signs awaited the disciplined David McKenna. Though his regimen called for three-mile runs, sometimes five miles, a monitored stress test in the clinic showed threatening blips on the screen. He went on high potency cholesterol medicine that worked, but all too well. He now suffered energy loss and a radical decline in motivation. He did not even want to face his assignments; worse, he did not care.

After examination at Mayo Clinic in Jacksonville, Florida, where he received skilled medical guidance, he recaptured his strength and zest for work and life. But an emotional crisis brought on by high stress coupled with awareness of his genetic inheritance brought him to his knees. Would he in fact live through his sixties? He did not know, but recommitted his life to God. He could live or die.

That fresh surrender resulted once more in the return of energy and excitement for family life and professional work. He did ever so much want to live long enough to retire with Janet, officiate at the weddings of all his children, and then watch his grandkids grow up.

At sixty-five years of age, out doing a four-mile run, David suddenly felt ill at ease. "My chest tensed up, my breath came short, and my arm felt like a ton of lead." Rest seemed to relieve the distress. On a subsequent run, however, the same serious trouble reoccurred. Even mowing the lawn brought on symptoms. Then as he watched television, the ominous signs appeared again. He knew he must act promptly. This time David ended up in the hospital, with nurses, doctors and equipment surrounding him.

A Reflective Pause in the Story

The original title of Dag Hammarskjöld's *Markings*, typed by him in his native Swedish, appeared as *Vägmärken* ("Trail Marks"). Hammarskjöld explains: "These notes?— They were signposts you began to set up after you had reached a point where you needed them, a fixed point that was on no account to be lost sight of." He referred to his mountain-climbing experiences. On treks, he piled up stones as markers of progress in uncharted mountain terrain. The stones also helped him find his way down the mountain, and assisted future hikers who might go the same route sometime later. "Perhaps it may be of interest to somebody," comments Dag Hammarskjöld, "to learn about a path about which the traveler who was committed to it did not wish to speak while he was alive." The result? *Markings*, the now famous spiritual journey written by the late secretary general of the United Nations. *Markings* is the diary the great man kept, which was published posthumously.

In much the same way, David McKenna has written about the spiritual and medical milestones of his cardiac challenges in his engaging little book, *Journey Through a By-pass* (Light and Life Communications, 1998).

Return to the Journey

Angioplasty alleviated the 95-percent-blocked left coronary artery. After a twenty-four-hour rest, David was sent home, with the echo of the doctor's words in his ears: "We'll know in a few months if the angioplasty holds. If it does, it's usually good for two and a half to three years."

David found himself holding life lightly. Though he wanted very much to live, he began to anticipate mortality in earnest. The Pauline passage, "For to me, to live is Christ and to die is gain" (Philippians 1:21, NIV), took a new hold on him. One recalls Elizabeth Kubler-Ross's findings in her researches on death: the one who truly faces death releases himself or herself to live fully in the present life. David made that discovery for himself.

Two days after angioplasty, he returned to the road, walking two miles without pain. Then a few days later he went back to the five-mile-a-day routine, though now he must carry nitroglycerin. "I found the protection of my youthful spirit, my optimistic outlook and my childlike faith inadequate for the new experience." He had never seen himself as over the hill at forty, nor had he suffered a midlife crisis at fifty; even in retirement, he imagined himself going on forever.

All the threats that invaded his mind in crisis created a mood of extreme difficulty in facing his new challenge. "Someday, sooner than I would like, I must die. How do I cope?" Then David recalled Jesus' words, " . . . do not worry about tomorrow, for tomorrow will worry about itself" (Matthew 6:34, NIV).

Now somewhat adjusted to the new reality, he began to sing. And the Lord gave him both lyrics and a tune—all his own—for a new praise chorus:

I sing of Thee, O Christ my Savior,
I sing of Thee, O Christ my Lord.
For each new day that You will give me,
I give it back so joyfully.

God showed him a simple but profound truth: what years he had left he must live fully and joyfully. The famous words of Jesus appeared on the screen of his mind with new vibrancy: "I have come that they may have life, and have it to the full" (John 10:10, NIV).

David's praying heart lifted praise, reflecting a still deeper adjustment to the realization that he, like all of us, are terminal cases. "To receive every waking moment as a gift from God, let Him fill it up with meaning, and give it back to Him with gratitude and for His glory." He concludes his musings with a flash of fresh insight: " . . . this was a benefit of redemption that I had missed."

David now composed a prayer to encapsulate his newfound joy in living. It goes like this:

"Lord of the Youthful Spirit—I cannot stop my body from aging, but I can stay young in mind and spirit. May I grow old singing a song that celebrates the newness of life. In the name of Him who walked the road with joy. Amen."

The Next Challenge

Almost two and a half years to the day after the angioplasty, it gave way. David's warning came while playing tennis. Of course he popped a nitro tablet. He continued hitting balls and running about the court. In the days ahead, he did the same, even playing several sets at a time. A new stress test, however, now ordered by the doctor, revealed abnormalities in the heart.

What a time to have a problem! The family had planned a vacation at Lake Chelan where they had had their get-togethers for twenty-eight years. Even more, Rob, David and Janet's youngest, would marry just after the vacation period. Obviously, David did not want to go through a hospital experience until vacation and wedding had come full circle.

However, more tests revealed two blocked arteries. Caught in a time crunch, Janet and David decided in thirty seconds to go ahead with open-heart surgery. Angioplasty again would have served as only a temporary respite. The vacation at the lake never came off. David hoped now that he could recover in time for Rob's wedding.

Sons Doug and Rob arrived at the hospital to stand by their dad; David's two daughters held standby tickets in case they needed to come to their father's bedside. The patient confessed his fears openly. But the family, ever supportive, prayed, read Scripture, and assured him he must go through with the surgery.

Surgery at Last

The anesthesiologist appeared and said, "I've read your history, and I see that you got your warning on the tennis court. Are you a religious man?"

"I try to be," the hospital patient answered.

"Well," the doctor announced, "if you are, you should thank your God because you dared Him to take your life!"

Four hours of surgery followed. Wife and sons first met David's eyes when he awoke. He looked at the long incision down his chest. The nurse quipped, "Welcome to the Zipper Club!"

The surgery had gone well, but the doctor added an ominous note when he said, "We'll know in an hour if he has had a stroke!" The stroke never came as it does on some occasions, but it frightened David and the whole family, for standing with the family was his sister, one arm hanging limp due to her own recent stroke.

All sighed with relief when at last David came through the whole affair unscathed by stroke or serious side effects. But four days in the hospital proved not so good. The food, for one thing, did not come up to low-cholesterol standards. The embarrassed nurse apologized for the dietary department of the hospital.

To avoid self-preoccupation during convalescence, David read a stimulating book, something he loves doing. Time passed, and the proud father officiated at Rob's beautiful wedding. Then, two months later, David and Rob flew to Cairo, Egypt, where David led a visioning conference for Free Methodist missionaries. Later still, he said yes to an invitation from the Overseas Council to help in a leadership development project for presidents of graduate schools of theology.

The Challenges Don't Let Up

Recently David has suffered what physicians call "Sjogren's-like disease." Symptoms include dry mouth, fiery tongue, and facial tingling. Doctors say symptoms may ulti-mately point to a systemic disease more definitely diagnosed. Tests include lip biopsy and a difficult MRI.

Billy Graham, longtime friend of David McKenna, wrote a feeling letter:

Dear David,

I just heard that you are going through a difficult time physically, and wanted you to know of our prayers.

As you go through the tests, biopsy, MRI, etc., we pray for wisdom for the doctors and nurses and for grace and strength for you.

Ruth and I have been struggling with our own health problems—my longtime board member, Allan Emery, said that these are not the "Golden Years" but the "Rusty Years." I think as we are all getting older we are more surprised than perhaps we should be as we encounter all these situations. It isn't easy, is it? And yet we know that we serve a mighty God who is faithful to keep His promise to hold our hand in His as we walk down the road.

With warmest Christian greetings, and appreciation for all that you mean to the Kingdom of God.

Cordially,
Billy

David's reply shows his warm and friendly sentiments:

Dear Billy and Ruth:

What a wonderful gift of grace to hear from you. Billy, God has now lengthened the cords of your anointed ministry to include encouragement as well as evangelism. Forgive me for slipping into the vernacular, but "You made my day!!" Thanks again and again.

My mysterious symptoms have escaped the scrutiny of two MRIs, twenty-five blood tests, a spinal tap, and one nasty lip biopsy. We rejoice in the fact that life-threatening and de-bilitating diseases have been ruled out, so God has given us the bounce to go on living with the freedom and the fullness of His grace. My face feels like a mask of nerves and my mouth feels as if I am constantly sucking a persimmon, but both are manageable so far.

As you know so well, we may retire from career, but we never retire from ministry . . . .

My days are more than full with writing a book a year, editing the forthcoming Christian Family Library, and chairing the Board of Trustees at Spring Arbor College in Michigan. Like you, the "rust" has to catch up with me and the "gold" still shines through.

With the fullness of His joy,
David

Robinson Crusoe—The Metaphor

Daniel Defoe pictures Robinson Crusoe as both a lonely, isolated islander and an overcomer *par excellence*. His unusual circumstances did not rule him; he ruled them. He grew a garden, raised goats, made a boat. He found help in his servant, Friday. Threatened by cannibals, he fought and cleverly worked his way to safety. Repeated threats could not stop him.

Defoe portrays Robinson with knowledge of God and His Word. Do we wonder that he came through it all victoriously?

THE COMMUNICATOR
Getting Through

The two words "information" and
"communication" are often used
interchangeably, but they signify
quite different things.
Information is giving out;
communication is getting through.
—Sydney J. Harris

THE COMMUNICATOR:
Getting Through

The legend of the Pied Piper of Hamelin is set in a charming little German town marked by winding, narrow streets and picturesque overhanging gables. The town had problems. The Pied Piper played his instrument and, much to everyone's amazement, the problems went away. The piper also spoke with firm conviction, making truth unforgettably vivid. More, he captured his audience and people followed him.

The people of Hamelin—since known as Hameln—celebrate the legend of the communicator of their village to this day as children read the Grimm Brothers' story. The town features a Pied Piper museum, and the narrative is written on a wall in the marketplace. Best of all, twice daily, to the accompaniment of the glockenspiel, a piper walks around the clock tower, musical pipe to his mouth, children following.

Modern Hameln celebrates what we all celebrate—the genius of communication that winsomely penetrates minds and hearts.

The Magic of Getting Through

Listen to David McKenna or read his writings and very quickly you recognize his ability to penetrate to the heart of things. He can engage your mind with a crucial issue, analyze it, and then bring the whole together—much as one does a puzzle—into an "ah-ha" moment of realization. "There it is!" you say to yourself. "Now I see the whole picture."

German psychologists named such an "ah-ha" experience a *gestalt*. With David McKenna the communicator, a picture may come together with an incisive word, a sentence or extended comment—this after giving the background, laid out winsomely and vividly. Sometimes the last piece of the puzzle falls into place with a bit of wit, often couched in the most delightful and insightful humor. Whether by a story, a one-liner or a sword-thrust observation, David McKenna knows how to "wrap things up," with everyone recognizing his creativity and ability to come to grips with reality and do something about it.

When the Pied Piper plays, the message gets through.

The Gift of Integration

An educator commented, "Dr. McKenna is fun to listen to." Yes, because of his ability to see ahead, to picture in advance of his audience both the problem at hand and the solution. The painting, however, never comes to completion without a lot of work. It happens rather much like an artist making preliminary pencil sketches before applying paint to canvas, a novelist watching characters take on a life of their own as the work emerges or a composer sketching notes on a musical score pad in preparation for creating a sonata. That's the work behind the finished product, behind the integrated whole, behind the completed portrayal.

One seldom sees David McKenna without his long yellow legal pad. He listens and records impressions with the speed of light. He also reads with the appetite of a hungry boy coming into dinner after football. All the while, he exercises his gift of observing, analyzing, testing—all in the interest of creating a completed image. So habitual is this life-of-the-mind style that he quickly sees the genius point in a plan, then capitalizes on it to bring persuasion to climax.

The Art of Persuasion

Not that persuasion always comes easily. A young man, devoting his life to public communication, tackled McKenna in an advisory meeting where an upcoming publication was under discussion. McKenna had argued for sequential communication, using a worship experience to illustrate his point. "Last Sunday," David began, "I attended a well-known church with a large modern audience. What interested me," he continued, "came as a bit of a surprise. The many young people in the congregation listened avidly and looked carefully at the outline of the sermon on the overhead screen."

At once the tackler retorted, "People don't think that way anymore. They do not follow a speaker in straight lines; they think in sound bytes, not necessarily related."

The sequel to the dialogue fascinated us all. McKenna answered not a word; he had already made his point. When the publication under examination emerged, it had harmony, not cacophony; clearly the writers and workers on the project saw meaning in sequence and relationships, in reasoned presentation.

Well, yes. Otherwise, will anyone be persuaded?

Classical Disciplines

Writers on communication tell us nature provides human beings with three primary vehicles for getting through: words (semantics), tone (tonics) and body language (kinesics). David McKenna has carefully developed skills in all three areas.

David knows the value of words, and before any public address writes until he has couched his ideas in clear, understandable language suitable to his audience. One needs only to sit behind him on a platform to see his intentionality at wordsmithing. He takes a full manuscript to the pulpit or podium, having highlighted in transparent color the key words and phrases, making certain he projects exact meanings.

Precision marked his work even from his early years in ministry and public life. He came to Seattle Pacific College in the late 1950s to do a spiritual life week. Then president of

Spring Arbor College in Michigan, he focused intentionally on his Seattle Pacific sermons, refusing to allow himself very much attention to his duties in Michigan. He sat at a desk poring over the addresses, changing a word here, revising there, rephrasing in language with optimal appeal to college students. His goal: to write himself clear, unmistakably lucid, while at the same time sharing substance.

The marriage of words to tone brings to McKenna's public speech a most remarkable synergism. One could create ever-so-careful language, yet fail to communicate effectively because vocal expression lacks life. Monotone turns people off, but David never creates Dullsville! His inviting and flexible tonal qualities draw people to rapt attention. Tone matches meaning.

Dr. McKenna can come across as firm, unequivocal in moral, ethical and professional conviction. His very tone, when preaching about sin or compromise, lets listeners know he means business about "sin, righteousness, and the judgment." He can also have fun with his audiences, bringing peals of laughter, or the pleasantry that invites one, sometimes ever so gently, at other times ever so hilariously, to say yes to truth.

Body language can indeed communicate. A look of the eyes can also communicate firmness, conviction or pleasantry. And that we must look at in more detail.

Elton Trueblood, the influential Quaker, had just spent time with Dr. McKenna at Seattle Pacific University. "He knows how to handle himself," said Dr. Trueblood to me. I pondered that single quick sentence, marked by the economy typical of the Friends. Trueblood meant that McKenna brought all his skills to the communication enterprise, grooming his whole self, including the bodily action that carries messages.

The relation of careful apparel, image and body language carries enormous weight in the effectiveness of communication—research says 65 percent to 80 percent of a total communication event. Stance, conservative use of gestures, and the intentional look—all work in concert to produce intended effect. Having taught drama when a high school teacher, McKenna knows the impact of bodily action in public speaking. He understands, too, the varied roles of public communicators.

The Man and His Audience

Much of this collective knowledge comes to him intuitively. He just seems to know the varied communication styles, whether in committee, chairing a board meeting, preaching a sermon or addressing a group of educators such as the United Methodist University Senate. He appears not to be merely studying role-playing; he knows simply that he must make himself acquainted with the audience in its environment.

This helps to explain the range of levels of communication in which he engages. He can sit with his grandchildren and read *The Little Engine That Could,* or talk to his adult children about their professions. He can engage in a dinner discussion about contemporary issues, sharing in-depth knowledge, both insightful and informational. Or he can enter dialogue about the culture, addressing the challenges of postmodernism. He can also as easily hold forth in sophisticated discussion about educational theory.

Whatever the setting, he embraces themes that fit, knowing how to bring words, tone and body language together to create communication that engages his listeners.

A Price to Pay

In a culture where articulate speech is scarce, good public address turns some people off. I remember a seminarian who dropped out of my communications class, and then out of seminary, declaring, "I don't like exact speech." Well, not only a young fellow trying to find himself, but also professional people, knowing the advantages of "being a communicator," may feel a sense of threat. Research indicates an almost one-to-one relationship between public speech ability and leadership. Yet, not many leaders have honed their verbal skills.

An educator tackled David one day, complaining, "You are so articulate." Well, yes, but this is a gift few enjoy. David faces the threat he knows he brings to some hearers. Fortunately, he does not recoil from the communication graces God bestowed on him.

Others feel threatened not because they themselves cannot speak so well, but because of the fast-track way his mind works. I have heard him speak publicly about that; he identifies with the slower, process people in his audiences, yet does not throw in the towel. He knows enough listeners track with him to sense his thrill of excitement. He also knows that some more deliberate processors, moving at their own pace, will become the most productive in helping him execute his dreams.

Joy and Humor

"A note of joy . . . from David L. McKenna" appears at the top of his stationery. He often closes his letters and e-mails with, "With His Joy." I know of no one who enjoys a good story or a bit of pleasantry more than Dave McKenna does. He's just fun to be with.

That spirit of gladness and fun comes right through in his public addresses. He loves to tell the story, for example, of the college educator who introduced—or attempted to introduce—Billy Graham's brother-in-law, Leighton Ford. To the students in the chapel the usually dignified and precise master of ceremonies declared, "We are happy to have Leighton Ford as our guest speaker this morning. Perhaps some of you don't know that Leighton Ford is married to Billy Graham's brother." Students began to titter, but the dis-

tinguished man, unaware of his mistake and looking non-plussed, added, "That makes Leighton Billy Graham's son-in-law." By this time the students could contain themselves no longer. The presiding officer tried desperately to fix whatever must have gone wrong, only to fail miserably with these words: "So now, I present to you, Leighton Ford's brother-in-law, Billy Graham."

Dave loves that story and says he feels ever so glad he was not the emcee! In humor lies one of the grand secrets of David McKenna's power as a communicator. He understands the effectiveness of mirth, that some truths transmit in humor what cannot come across with success in straightforward language. One simply cannot join him for coffee without a good laugh. More than a clever device for managing life and speech—and it surely does help us cope!—laughter lives in the heart of the Christian. G. K. Chesterton, quoting St. Francis of Assisi, reminds us that we should let the devil be sad—he's got plenty to be sad about.

But the Christian! Ah, that's another story. Christians believe with unequivocal conviction in the empty tomb, and just there lies the theology behind the joy of the Christian communicator. The resurrected Christ, through His Spirit, lives in us, not merely as a nice idea, but in spiritual reality. ". . . Christ in you, the hope of glory," cries St. Paul in Colossians (1:27, NKJV). No wonder a Harvard psychologist says that if Christians really believe their faith they have every reason to laugh and express joy. Of course they do, for God, not evil, stands in charge of this world. So life's incongruities become the basis of mirth, and humor assists in creating a victorious attitude, and a Christian perspective restores clarity in the most trying of circumstances, and allows creative solutions for complex problems to emerge.

This stance explains why Dr. McKenna does not spend time talking very much about the evil in the world. He once told his presidential cabinet not to focus so much on the problems of the school. That stance irritates some academicians: how can we deal with challenges if we don't discuss them? they reason. Well, David confronts issues head on, but once "problem" talk has come full circle, he stops. He feeds his soul on the theological truth that declares God will win. This explains why one seldom hears him complaining, either in private or in public, neither in committee nor from the pulpit. The bottom line: he's a believer, and humor, the joy of the Lord which is strength (Nehemiah 8:10), testifies to resurrection faith.

The Role of the Spirit

Good diction, excellent vocal expression, telling body language, humor—all these gifts can serve the ego. That frightens David McKenna. Asked to do Bible studies at the Cove, Billy Graham's retreat center in the Carolinas, David became "really frightened," to use his own words, "when people paid too much attention to me." Did they respond to his public skills or to Christ?

Prayer, for David, opens the door to self-surrender of all his personal gifts in the sole interest of Kingdom objectives. He believes strongly the truth articulated by James Denney, the Scottish theologian, that a preacher shows either his own cleverness or the sovereign, saving Christ. David insists on sharing Christ; one's individual gifts must serve Him.

The release of those gifts in His interests comes by the power of the Holy Spirit. Precisely there lies the difference between the secular communicator and the Christian: the one examines the principles of rhetoric to learn techniques and strategies, the art, of getting through to people. David has no quarrel with educating persons to be good communicators. Speech, homiletics, drama—all the communication arts— have their place in the educational setting. In fact, he went out for oratory and debate in his high school years, and entered public speech contests too.

To stop with training, however, is an impossibility for the Christian communicator. Impossible, that is, if one genuinely wants to propagate gospel communication. One must lean on the Spirit of God to move the truth from the ear to the heart.

Martin Marty, longtime friend of David McKenna and recently retired from the divinity school of the University of Chicago, tells of sharing a platform with the almost blind Joseph Sittler, "a man who really saw, and heard." Someone asked the theologian Sittler, "If you had to reduce a call for reformation of the Church to one sentence, what would it say?" The great man's answer: "Watch your language."

David McKenna knows the power of words to engage people in Christian commitment and action: godly living, feeding the poor, showing kindness. He also knows that language, aside from the presence of God, falls on deaf ears. Prayer-saturated words empower not only the speaker but also the hearer.

The Range of Gospel Communication

Passionate about getting through to people, this Pied Piper pipes with pen as well as mouth. Perusing McKenna's many volumes, one notices immediately the sheer range of his work. Believing the pen mightier than the sword, he tackles issues, writing with the kind of cutting edge that characterizes communicators of our time like Maxie Dunnam, Charles Colson, and Leonard Sweet. One could wish for a wider circulation of his books; he jokes about sales and gives many of his books away. But sometimes a limited distribution means a select readership, readers who can and will make a difference in the world.

In the Word Books publication *Renewing Our Ministry*, McKenna declares his conviction that no higher calling exists than the Christian ministry. He speaks of the imperative of new birth, of nurturing relationships, of keeping alert to the contemporary culture and of assuming the servant role as the prerequisite for ministerial leadership. Ever the interested missioner, he cannot overlook the cross-cultural revolution of our time; we *must* get the gospel out and do it with the aid of the findings of culture studies. More, McKenna pleads for renewal in ministry. Listen to his plea: ". . . the purpose of this book is singular. *God in Christ, through His Holy Spirit, has precommitted all of the resources we need for the renewal of our ministry* . . . My prayer is that every minister of the gospel who reads this book will kneel in the presence of God, claim the promises for renewal and rise with an energizing gleam in the eye given by the Spirit of God" (xii).

As one looks at McKenna's writing, one cannot miss his awareness of both history and contemporary society; the gospel worker must show keen awareness of both to minister effectively. The resurrection of our Lord, for example, took place in history and carries enormous present-day implications for abiding in the Spirit and therefore living victoriously. The Holy Spirit, who came at Pentecost at a point in time and is still present now, makes it possible to cope with the crosscurrents in today's world.

In *Megatruth* David McKenna reminds us that the Holy Spirit teaches us how to live today—righteously, meaningfully, creatively, morally, effectively—in a chaotic, mind-boggling culture in radical transition. "Megatrends need megatruth," declares McKenna. He goes on: "The church of Jesus Christ is entrusted with the final and authoritative Word of God and we have been promised the continuing application of truth through the Spirit of God. Working together through the mind of the believer and the message of the church, the Word and the Spirit teach us, correct us, and direct us as we face the trends of the times. Therefore, in the Age of Information when truth is up for grabs, the church is just coming into its own" (p. 17).

In all this McKenna speaks to both professional clergy

and laypeople. Church, mission and ministry all come together in potent, penetrating language.

Writing for the Poor in Spirit

Part of the dynamic of his broad audience relates to concern for the poor, the hurting, and the suffering. Over and again in his works, we see these motifs. He carries genuine concern – empathy – for persons in distress. For example, in *The Whisper of His Grace,* a spin-off from his *Communicator's Commentary on Job,* he sees hope for human beings caught in the clutches of original sin, and documents from Scripture that God's grace translates catastrophe into celebration. Job illustrates that divine principle. "Only human beings can ask 'Why?'" McKenna observes with both realism and empathy. "Created in the image of God, it is our nature to reflect upon our suffering, put it into the perspective of experience, and pose questions that probe into the very heart of human experience" (p. 17).

An optimist, McKenna refuses to wallow in the dust of crisis, but asks the courageous question: Since we live in a very bad world, why don't more bad things happen? His answer: God's Presence puts limits on evil. Grace does in fact act in the lives of His people.

The Whisper of His Grace is so exciting, so relevant, not only because we have here a preacher who faces fully the awesome "whys" of life—all centered in why God does not stop evil—but also because of McKenna's refreshing reminder of the power of grace. Whys find an answer in Who—God himself, walking with us in our sadness, and granting us the further grace of freedom from bitterness. In all his discussions of the hurts of people, we see the balance that psychological training brings, and the theological perspective that a suffering Christ and His cross lends to the difficult questions.

Jesus the Model, Scripture the Textbook

Always, Jesus is the model for David McKenna; this explains why He shows up so often on printed pages. If McKenna writes about human behavior, Jesus is the hero. If David wrestles with helping people emotionally and spiritually, Jesus stands in all His power as the One to emulate. A couplet appears in several of his writings and is heard often in his public addresses. It expresses how he sees theology as looking and reaching both ways—heavenward to Jesus and outward to a hurting world:

Passion for One,
Compassion for all.

Even as Jesus is the model human being, so the Bible is the primary textbook for learning how to put into practice what we see in Christ. McKenna shows his understanding of this truth in his extensive commentaries in the *Communicator's* series edited by Lloyd Ogilvie. Not only did David write the *Communicator's Commentary on Job,* he also did the two volumes on the book of Isaiah, and the one on Mark. The genius of the *Communicator's Commentary* lies in its right-brain orientation. Truths come to life in stories and pictures.

McKenna's View of Scripture

David McKenna sees Scripture as the rule of faith and practice, and in this he follows the evangelical tradition of the Christian church. The recorded and divine revelation, Scripture holds the place of primacy, the place of supreme-written authority. The Scripture becomes dominant for him, for both preaching and teaching, for discussion and published writing. He identifies with the universal witness of the church through the ages, that the Bible, by its inward witness, authenticates itself. Other writings do not hold the same authenticity nor does church tradition, as important as that is, and certainly not individual revelations like dreams, visions and personal messages. The Bible stands alone, against the culture, and is even over the individual conscience since human beings can in fact suffer from false conditionings.

How does Christ fit into this high view of Scripture? For starters, the Bible witnesses of Christ; it is our primary source of information about Him. More, we cannot worship a book (bibliolatry); we can only worship a Person, the Person of Jesus Christ, the Son of God. In a summary sentence, one that comes out of the centuries-long tradition of the church universal, "Christ is King and Lord of Scripture." This statement identifies the bedrock that underlies McKenna's writing, speaking, living.

The Theological Basis of Communication

What, then, of McKenna's theology? The driving force of his communication, written and oral?

After Christ himself and the Holy Trinity, personal salvation stands at the top of any list. One must be born again (John 3). That determines the kind and quality of relationship with God and with human beings. David's own vivid conversion experience, outlined in the first chapter, constitutes the experiential basis of his strong belief about new birth.

Salvation, he believes, comes by grace alone. And McKenna simply cannot stop talking about grace. You see it in his books; you hear it in his addresses. This accounts for his realistic assessment of himself and his gifts, and explains in part his native shyness. He stands amazed that God would choose and use him, a Tabernacle kid. He feels he really does not deserve the adulation he often gets. And sometimes he confesses blunders. I once heard him say after delivering an address, "It was a terrible speech." Yet, he goes right on, never wavering, never stopping, so vividly real is the grace of God for him. And David McKenna wants everyone else to live in its joy and release.

Salvation, then, initial and ongoing, comes solely from God himself through grace. McKenna celebrates it with deep gratitude. Even more, just as salvation comes by grace alone, it also arrives through faith alone. Nor do we manufacture faith; only God can give faith, and here we are, once more, right back to grace. Grace alone provides faith. All we must do is exercise it, like a muscle. None of us gives ourselves muscles, but we can allow our strength to deteriorate by lack of exercise, or build and maintain it by lifting weights and running and swimming. David exercises physically; he also exercises his spiritual muscles. The discipline of the devout heart comes in for its part in his life. He studies the Word of God, prays, participates in the Christian community, and reads. He has recently completed a book on salient Christian literature and the devotional classics, and made recommendations of spiritual books everyone ought to know.

We can summarize Dr. McKenna's view of salvation in historic, classical terms:

Sola gratia = by grace alone

Sola fide = by faith alone

Sola Christus = by Christ alone

Herein lies basic theology and motivation for communication.

The Pied Piper Once More

The legend of the Pied Piper is just that, legend. It's a fairy tale for children. Some historians think an incident, perhaps the Children's Crusade of 1212, may have given rise to the story. We do not know. This we do know: the "magic" stands as a superb metaphor for communication that gets through.

The "magic" of David McKenna, and all gospel communicators who "get through," depends not solely on personal gifts and graces; primarily, it relies on the power of the Spirit and the content of the message. For David McKenna, both the power and the message can be summarized in three grand terms: *Christ, Holy Spirit* and *Bible.* Couple the Christian substance of McKenna's message, spoken and written, with God's gifts in him, and we witness a remarkable contemporary communicator. A Pied Piper of our time.

THE WORKER
To the Glory of God

"I never knew a man to work so intently."
—David Bundy at the opening of the
David L. McKenna Papers, B. L. Fisher Library,
Asbury Theological Seminary, Wilmore, Kentucky

THE WORKER:
To the Glory of God

Musa Alami of Lebanon suffered the loss of everything he had because of a military skirmish and ended up living in the desert. Though thriving Jericho was not far away, Musa and his family found themselves where they could live only with great difficulty, for no water existed. Mountains graced Musa's view on either side of the valley. The River Jordan might provide water for the sun-drenched valley if only he could find money to build a dam. Musa was a dreamer.

Research taught him about wells and under-the-surface waterways, and he determined to dig. Imagine the laughter, the jeering, the absolutely incredulous neighbors! "Don't you know the Dead Sea once covered this valley floor?" someone asked. "Don't you know about the salt-saturated earth here?" another queried. All with one voice cried, "You fool!"

But with vision and persistence Musa hired help. He began the dig with just men and shovels. The workers burrowed through sand and mineral, down, down, down, week upon week, for six months.

Then—water! Good water and lots of it.

Friends, neighbors, government officials did not laugh then. They cried for joy and saw enormous possibilities for making the desert valley into a place to live and developing farms rich in crops.

An Unstoppable Worker

Like Musa, once David McKenna gets an idea, creates a design, sees a clear goal, secures support to bring his vision to reality—once he lays the groundwork—nothing stops him. He does whatever he needs to do to bring a project to fruition.

This explains how college, university and seminary curricula came into place, and how teaching faculty came together to make possible the best in education. It explains how books and articles move from the study table to the publisher's desk. It reveals how addresses, framed in rich imagination, come to reality at the podium. It tells us how buildings move from idea to blueprint to donor to final physical reality.

Roadblocks abound for determined, creative people. David knows, as every visionary must, that with great ideas come great challenges, some of them formidable. Would his dream of an integrated curriculum at Spring Arbor College become reality? Would he ever get financing for the School of Business facility at Seattle Pacific University? What if the Beeson money for the seminary did not materialize?

When the digging for the quadrangle campus at Asbury took place, workers knew they had to drill through hard rock, but they did not expect to find an underground lake! Now what? An enormous concrete, steel-enforced bridge had to be constructed to cover the water. Such an expense! Such a headache for Eugene Lintemuth, the seminary's business manager! But with David's ever-optimistic and contagious spirit, architects, engineers and construction people were inspired to find a way. Humor entered the picture, too. One morning when David came to work, he saw a sign over the watery area: "McKenna Lake."

Yes, the foundation came to successful completion, and the problem lake? Really an advantage. Engineers developed protection for two enormous wells that would keep the campus green during the worst drought in more than 100 years during the summer and fall of 1999. And since the water belongs to the seminary, no city water fees!

Problems? Yes. Lots of them. People challenges too? Often. David has faced them. In a recent *Leadership Journal* cartoon, a pastor sits at his desk with a cup of coffee. His secretary reads off the morning's schedule that goes something like this: At nine you meet skepticism, at ten resistance and at noon ridicule and derision.

On the village church wall at Staunton, England, appear these telling words: "In this year 1653, when all things sacred were throughout the nation destroyed or profaned, this church was built to the glory of God by Sir Robert Shirley whose singular praise it was to have done the best of things in the worst of times." The same could be written of McKenna on the foundation of Asbury's quadrangle.

Conditioning from Childhood

David's robust work ethic strikes anyone who associates with him for very long. It all started in childhood. He learned to shoulder responsibility from his parents, both hard workers. In depression years Dad McKenna lost his Greyhound bus job. Did that stop him? Never. He proceeded to apply for work until he found a job in the auto-manufacturing world. At General Motors he became affectionately known as "Mac."

As a boy, David sold the *Saturday Evening Post* and *Country Gentleman* magazines, had a paper route at age twelve, worked in a hardware store, and made deliveries for a dry-cleaning establishment. Never without a job while growing up, he always found gainful employment. Work built fiber into him; it contributed to the development of his character; it gave him the ability to carry through no matter how he felt or how great the temptation to throw in the towel. He did his work faithfully, performing at his best level, not just to meet the requirements of his employers but also to go beyond expectations. This created in him a sense of pride in achievement.

Childhood conditioning set the pattern for life. During college days, hard work marked the industrious McKenna.

While finishing his bachelor of arts degree at Western Michigan University, he pastored a church, gave attention to family life, and paid his tuition. In seminary, he did manual labor for the school. For example, he helped in the construction of Estes Chapel, laboring in the high corners of the building, many feet above the ground. He also kept a vegetable garden to provide food for his growing family.

David McKenna gravitated toward work and did it conscientiously.

The à Kempis Quartet

Thomas à Kempis describes the dedicated person as, "Never to be completely idle, but either reading, or praying, or meditating, or working at something useful for all in common." That fourfold spiritual description of work—reading, praying, meditating, working at something useful—marks David McKenna.

1) *Reading.* Asbury Theological Seminary Provost Robert Mulholland read a book so fresh and creative that he passed it on to President McKenna, who took the volume with him to a speaking engagement. Though he had prepared his address, after reading the book on the airplane he rewrote his talk. Never shying away from the hard labor of revision, even a complete rewrite, McKenna lives with excitement on the growing edge of discovery.

One never sees David without a book. He loves sharing his findings. He knows the power of research to inform the mind, trigger creativity, and enrich communication. Go into his office or home and see books—journals and magazines, too. He keeps his mind sharp and clear and helps others find stimulating literature, exhorting friends to read the best materials. The work of meaningful reading stems from the earliest days in boyhood, at elementary school, and in and out of high school. As he moved through training, he won scholarships. He demonstrated knowledge and used information to strengthen class discussions and later in life to create and enhance curricula and academic program building.

The motivation to read also has roots—actually the most important roots—in his love and knowledge of the Bible. He understands that American higher education got its impetus from the Scriptures. David has made a lifetime study of God's Word and is well aware of the Bible's messages about the life of the mind. He has lived out the biblical focus on learning which Acts 2:42 describes: "And they devoted themselves to the apostles' teaching and fellowship, to the breaking of bread and the prayers" (RSV). How interesting that the first of the four items relates to education and signals the role of teaching! For David McKenna, reading becomes one of the key factors in ongoing learning, and he works through volumes of books and articles with excitement, joy, and a sense of creative involvement.

The book of Proverbs, which is saturated with words like *teaching, wisdom* and *insight*, heralds the life-giving benefits of learning. David labors intensively at the learning enterprise and generously passes on his findings.

2) *Praying.* Dr. McKenna's training in home, church and Christian institutions of higher learning taught him that the way Christians get their work done is by prayer. Prayer *is* work.

Norman Edwards served as an administrator at Seattle Pacific University with David McKenna. "My most prized memories of working with Dave," Norm reflected, "are the times we prayed together in his office about students in special need." This readiness to pause in the day's activity for intercession stems from his personal and private devotional life. Open Bible, devotional books, prayer—often with pad and pen at hand—form the well from which problems find solution and ideas come to birth. The quiet time is a must in David's routine.

McKenna believes so thoroughly in the devout life that

he has produced an entire volume, *How to Read a Christian Book*, to give direction for Christlike living. So vividly does he see prayer as motivation and guidance that he must publish in bold print, as it were, the grand principles of intercession, principles made clear and vividly illustrated in the lives and teaching of the fathers and spiritual leaders of church history.

Praying takes on many expressions in David's life: private prayers, small-group intercession, petitions for direction at the outset of a committee meeting, praise and prayer in public worship, and of course family prayers. In all the praying, he knows that praise frames requests that God answers. That explains why one never hears him grumble or engage in self-pity, either in tone or in word. God talks to the joyous, believing soul. So the work of prayer is not tedious or laborious so much as inspiring and nurturing. This established principle means that all of life has potential for being prayer. Like the seventeenth-century French monk Brother Lawrence, whether one does the dishes in the kitchen or kneels at the Holy Communion table, God's presence is the same. The Divine Presence marks David's life with its lilt and song in the midst of arduous effort and daily toil. This accounts for the dynamic behind the productivity of his life.

3) *Meditating.* A Hebrew word for meditation means—well, picture a rolling snowball going down hill gathering snow. Meditation is the work of processing, rolling an idea over and over again, letting it accumulate sub-ideas and possibilities until the original concept comes to its intended full size.

Dr. McKenna knows how to process ideas. They begin in prayer, listening to God, dialoging with the Divine. Then, also under the aegis of divine leadership, the ideas develop into a picture. Once the picture forms clearly, at least specifically enough to present to others, David extends the processing procedure with group discussion. He does this first with a small group, then in a larger circle.

Someone once said of Bob Pierce, the founder of World Vision, that he threw away more ideas than most people have in a lifetime. Dr. McKenna is not far behind the creative Pierce. Like Pierce, McKenna discards ideas when he sees they will not work. Those mental pictures that do have the chance of becoming reality he processes over and again with individuals as well as groups. At the right time, the larger public has a chance to view the painting.

All that takes time, but it commences with meditation. Note where meditation comes in the quartet sequence—after reading and praying. À Kempis may not have recorded the four components of spiritual work in any premeditated order, but as it turns out, for McKenna reading and praying precede meditation, for they play their preliminary part in giving birth to an idea with potential. Meditative processing can and often does mean diligent labor, an exercise that may take years, but always enough time to get the job done.

4) *Working at something useful.* Dave is an inveterate worker. He cannot stop. Some have accused him of being a workaholic (a term invented by Wayne Oates, a pastoral care seminary professor and later professor of psychiatry at University of Louisville School of Medicine). When he goes to the beach, he takes his computer and writes books and articles. When he rides an airplane, he takes a book. When he drives in a car with friends, he often talks shop and processes ideas. Even David's recreation is work. I have seen him play tennis with the intentionality of a portrait painter making sure every detail on the canvas comes to accurate expression. When he jogs, he does it with focused attention.

All of David's life comes couched in industry, albeit happy industry, seldom destroying the dimension of spontaneity. And that leads us to itemizing, selectively, several pictures of his ambitious and productive labor pattern.

Published Books

As you scan through the following list of published books, try to imagine the research, writing, rewriting, editing, and talking on the phone with editors and publishers. Notice also the scope of Dr. McKenna's writing: Christian social consciousness, psychology, Bible commentary, contemporary issues, ministry, theology, leadership, parenting, history, medicine, discipleship, holy living. And one more, work. Just there we must look briefly at David McKenna's book, *Love Your Work*.

We have already noticed that, with Thomas à Kempis, McKenna sees work in a spiritual context. In *Love Your Work*, the title of chapter four is "First Principle: Work Is Prayerful." Listen to David's personal prayer about work: "Lord, deliver me from the subtle and secular influence that steals the spiritual meaning from my daily work. Never let me forget that I am Your partner in creation every day. Amen" (p. 49). Prayer prepares us for toil and gives proper perspective to the day's efforts. More, planning comes with prayer, and prayer becomes a source of energy. No wonder David McKenna gives us a Christian ethic of work and a theology in which to frame our philosophy of labor. "To reconnect our daily work with biblical spirituality," he observes, "we must see work as a resource of creation waiting to be redeemed by those who believe. Once redeemed it becomes a means of grace" (p. 22).

Now for the array of books that documents both the willingness and implementation of his beliefs about work, the diligence that issues in published writing:

The Urban Crisis (Editor), Grand Rapids: Zondervan, 1969.

Awake, My Conscience! Winona Lake: Light and Life Press, 1977.

The Communicator's Commentary: Mark, Vol. 2. Waco: Word Books, 1982.

The Psychology of Jesus: The Dynamics of Christian Wholeness (formerly titled *The Jesus Model*). Waco: Word Books, 1985.

The Communicator's Commentary: Job, Vol. 12. Waco: Word Books, 1986.

Megatruth: The Church in the Age of Information. San Bernardino: Here's Life, 1986.

Renewing Our Ministry. Waco: Word Books, 1986.

The Whisper of His Grace. Waco: Word Books, 1987.

Power to Follow, Grace to Lead: Strategy for the Future of Christian Leadership. Dallas: Word Books, 1989.

Love Your Work! Wheaton: Victor Books, 1990.

The Coming Great Awakening: New Hope for the Nineties. Downers Grove: InterVarsity Press, 1990.

The Communicator's Commentary: Isaiah 1-39, Vol. 16A. Dallas: Word, 1993.

The Communicator's Commentary: Isaiah 40-66, Vol. 16B. Dallas: Word, 1994.

When Our Parents Need Us Most: Loving Care in the Aging Years. Harold Shaw Publishers, 1994.

A Future with a History: The Wesleyan Witness of the Free Methodist Church. Indianapolis: Light and Life, 1997.

Journey through a Bypass: The Story of an Open Heart. Indianapolis: Light and Life, 1998.

Growing Up in Christ: Realizing Our Spiritual Potential. Indianapolis: Light and Life, 1998.

What a time to Be Wesleyan! Proclaiming the Holiness Message with Passion and Purpose. Kansas City: Beacon Hill, 1999.

How to Read a Christian Book. Grand Rapids: Baker Book House, January 2001 (release date).

Major Magazines and Journals

The above is not the complete record of McKenna's published writing. There is more, in a variety of publication types: Christian, collegiate, academic, news, organizational, ecclesiastical, etc. Observe, too, the varied audiences: the secular reader, the ordinary layperson in the church, leaders, researchers. The following list of publications that have carried his work continues the documentation of his desire to labor diligently.

Action (magazine of The National Association of Evangelicals—regular column, "In the World")

Alumni Advance (Asbury Theological Seminary)

Asbury Herald

Board Wise
Christian Life
Christianity Today
College & University
Decision Magazine
Ecumenical Reporter
Eternity
The Falcon (Seattle Pacific University campus paper)
Herald of Holiness (Church of the Nazarene magazine)
Journal of Educational Research
Leadership
Light and Life (Free Methodist Church magazine)
Response
Seattle Pacific University Alumni Magazine and Bulletin
Stewardship Magazine
United Evangelical Action
U.S. News & World Report
Vital Speeches of the Day
The War Cry (Salvation Army magazine)
Wesleyan Advocate (Wesleyan Church magazine)

Representative Major Addresses

Known for his public address, Dr. McKenna works assiduously at the task of concept development for his talks, then researches them, and finally writes the material word for word. He never appears for a formal speech without a full manuscript. In the following list of significant presentations, observe once more the span of his efforts: he addresses scholars, students, denominational conferences, administrators, government personnel, Bible assemblies, teachers, and others.

"Academy of Christian Scholars." National Association of Evangelicals, Wheaton, Illinois, March 31, 1978.

"Altar and Market Place." Denver Association of Evangelicals, October 15, 1971.

"Altar and Market Place." General Conference of the Mennonite Church, Fresno, California, August 20, 1971.

"Alumni Luncheon." United Methodist General Conference, Louisville, Kentucky, May 12, 1992.

"Build-up or Burn-out." Fellowship of Evangelical Seminary Presidents Annual Renewal Conference, Seattle, Washington, April 16, 1972.

"Caesar and Christ." General Conference of the Mennonite Church, Fresno, California, September 19, 1971.

"Christ Alone for Our Salvation." Nairobi, Kenya, July 24, 1986.

"Christian College and Current Trends in Higher Education." The Wesleyan Higher Education Conference, June 3, 1972.

"Christian College DewLine for Church." 100th Annual Conference of the Brethren in Christ Church, Upland, California, July 3, 1970.

"Christian Higher Education: A Global Network." World Conference at Lausanne in Manila, Philippines, July 9-21, 1989.

"Christian Higher Education and Family Development." Continental Congress on the Family, St. Louis, Missouri, October 13-17, 1975.

"Christian Higher Education and World Evangelism: A Strategy for the Future." Lausanne in Switzerland, July 1974.

"Christian Higher Education Indispensable to the Future." National Association of Evangelicals Report in USA (for presentation to Bishop Tong in China, November 1981).

"Christian Mind: Freedom." National Association of Evangelicals, Seattle, Washington, April 9, 1975.

"Christian Teacher: Impact and Immortality." National Educators Fellowship, Warm Beach Camp, Stanwood, Washington, August 1, 1972.

"Church and Public Morality." National Association of Evangelicals, Philadelphia, Pennsylvania, April 22, 1968.

"Coming Great Awakening." Christian Holiness Association, Lexington, Kentucky, April 17, 1990.

"Concept for a Christian College," Spring Arbor College Series: "Change or Perish," "Alternatives for Action," "Christ and the College," and "Curriculum for Commitment." Spring Arbor, Michigan, 1963.

"Developing Creative Tension in the Christian College." The American Association of Evangelical Students, April 10, 1964.

"Educator in the Mass Media." Christian Educators Conference, Tulsa, Oklahoma, April 1, 1971.

"Effective Christian Leadership." 13th Annual Governor's Prayer Breakfast, Olympia, Washington, January 25, 1969.

"For Such a Time as This!" World Methodist Council, Lake Junaluska, North Carolina, July 1, 1989.

"Forgotten America." Association of American Colleges, Houston, Texas, January 1970.

"Future of Our Evangelical Past." National Association of Evangelicals Bicentennial Convention, February 25, 1976.

"Grading on American Education." National Association of School Boards, Seattle, Washington, April 1, 1974.

"Higher Education Tuition and Testimony." U.S. Senate Sub-Committee: Labor, Health, Education, Washington, D.C., March 30, 1971.

"Holiness and the Moral Crises of Our Times." Christian Holiness Association 110th Convention, St. Louis, Missouri, April 18, 1978.

"Home for Christian Education." National Association of Evangelicals National Congress, Chicago, Illinois, November 8, 1978.

"National Student Leadership Conference." President's Lunch in Washington, D.C., March 28, 1980.

"Our Evangelical Agenda." National Association of Evangelical Boards of Administration, Minneapolis, Minnesota, February 20, 1978.

"Redeeming Love." Billy Graham Training Center, The Cove, North Carolina, October 18-22, 1993.

"Stewards of the Mystery." National Association of Evangelicals Banquet, Phoenix, Arizona, March 8, 1990.

"Teacher as a Model." KCTS-TV Live, Edmonds, South Dakota, September 1, 1971.

"Visibility and Viability for Evangelical Christian Colleges." National Association of Evangelicals, April 13, 1972.

"What a Time to Be Alive!" World Methodist Council, Lake Junaluska, North Carolina, July 1, 1989.

"Witnessing Church in a Secular World." National Association of Evangelicals 26th Annual Conference, Philadelphia, Pennsylvania, April 23-25, 1968.

Musa Alami and J. S. Bach

We began this chapter with the Musa Alami story. That story, at once remarkable and true, stands as a metaphor of what a motivated laborer can accomplish. Today farms cover the massive Jordan River valley, once a fruitless desert.

But I find David McKenna reserved when someone compliments him on his achievements. He seems to feel he could have done more and better; he comes across as shy and not wanting to talk about accomplishments. What I see in both his book *Love Your Work* and in his attitude reminds me of the spirit of Johann Sebastian Bach. On an untouched manuscript page, Bach often wrote two letters: J.J., for *Jesu Juva*— "Jesus, help me." Sometimes he would record I.N.J., *In Nomine Jesu*— "In the name of Jesus." At the end of a completed composition, Bach routinely wrote S.D.G., *Soli Deo Gloria*— "To God alone be the glory." Every piece of music J. S. Bach put together he did with genuine spiritual motivation.

Every work David McKenna executes he does with spiritual incentive. People who know him and his work see S.D.G., *To God alone be the glory,* at the end of each completed task.

THE LEADER
Churchman *Par Excellence*

We need a baptism of clear seeing.
We desperately need seers who can see
through the mist—Christian leaders
with prophetic vision.
—A. W. Tozer

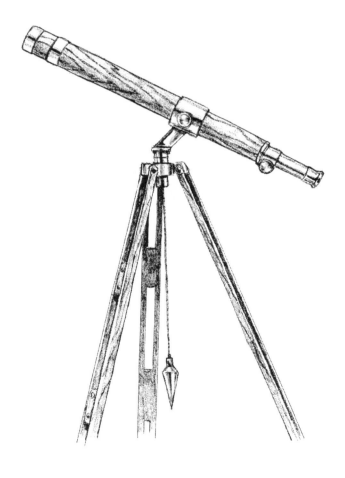

THE LEADER:
Churchman *Par Excellence*

A college exchange student, Elijah, sat at breakfast in a Moscow hotel near a group of rowdy clowns. They told Elijah they were doctors and clowns from various countries traveling with Patch Adams. "One of the talkative ladies half jokingly asked if I wanted to join them for the day," Elijah reported.

Late that afternoon, Elijah went back to the hotel to join them and met a tall male harlequin sporting long gray and blue hair in a ponytail. When Elijah asked about a costume, he discovered that the longhaired clown was none other than Patch Adams himself. The door opened to talk with the famous clown. When did Patch get interested in Russia? He'd been going to Russia for some seventeen years. What about religion? Patch "loves Jesus," but has never claimed Him as personal Savior or bought into faith and redemption.

Elijah's part of the group went to an orphanage. "This was my favorite part of the whole day . . . giving a little laughter and joy" to hurting and lonely people.

Bold Leadership with Joy

The Patch Adams story is analogous to the David McKenna story, with similarities and differences. David is no clown, but in his own way he capitalizes on the resources of laughter. Adams, full of fun by nature, knows the scientific and hormonal results and cures of laughter; McKenna runs on the joy of the Lord who is his strength. Adams works for the betterment of humankind on earth; McKenna labors to see both heaven and earth populated with Christians who will live out their faith. The one sees the stage and hospital as his vehicles for helping people; the other views the church of Jesus Christ as his means of mission. A strong vision for change characterizes them both. Each wants to see people helped beyond the ordinary.

Both work with a bold tenacity that sometimes makes the pillars of contemporary society shake. Patch Adams let the medical world know he would indeed find creative ways to help break down the "Berlin Wall" that prevented the poverty-stricken from receiving health care. He would even make fun of the wealthy doctors and their sophisticated, complex and protective ploys that prevented service to the poor. David McKenna would not so much make fun of the churches and schools with their set ways, as he would reveal the gospel as joyous good news to attract people of all walks and races. But he would shake up the "way it was always done," creating new methodologies and fresh perspectives.

The Making of a Leader

From his youth, David McKenna was a leader. He took leadership roles in his church youth group. He served as president and class historian in his senior year of high school; he was captain of his tennis team and also president of his senior class. Early training marked him an overseer. His peers recognized his gifts, and this in turn signaled to him that God had gifted him.

The ethical teaching of his church conditioned him to strict honesty. For example, as a lad he worked in a grocery store. One day he made off with a twenty-five-cent piece. His conscience got the better of him, and he had to return the quarter. Later, in a physics class, he cheated on an exam. Once more he knew he had to make amends. Still another time, he took money from a coffee can in which his dad kept the church money (his father served as church treasurer) in order to take care of his newspaper route bills. (Some of his customers did not pay their bills on time.) David returned the money to the coffee can.

Not only did David learn at an early age that integrity marks Christian leaders, he also discovered that they must work harder than those they lead. Diligence constitutes a significant part of his incarnational theology of leadership. How can one expect others to follow if their leader himself does not pitch in for all he's worth?

Undergirding the whole leadership formation experience, David sees his conversion at an early age and his filling of the Spirit in seminary as the spiritual power behind creative and productive supervision. From those two defining experiences has come one moment of grace after another – heading committees, supervising organizations, and serving institutions. Those duties, along with mentoring individuals who are seeking God's best, require heaven's help.

While Patch Adams has given leadership to the health-care community, David McKenna has provided it for the church with its spiritual potential.

Working Principles

Bishop M. D. Ormston ordained McKenna in 1952. He remembers racing through the questions until the bishop came to the question, "Are you in debt?" Unexpectedly, David answered yes and "blew all of the fuses in the system!" The bishop swallowed hard and then, perhaps remembering that David had just finished college, asked, "Is it such that you can manage it?" The ordinand corrected himself and assured the bishop that his answer should have been no.

Ordination opened the door wide for pastoring, evangelistic opportunity, pulpit work, denominational guidance, as well as higher education. Though college settings provided the laboratory for him to put into practice his managerial gifts, he has always seen himself as working for the church and the kingdom of God.

1) ***The primacy of vision.*** The first task of the leader, says Dr. McKenna, is to define reality. To evaluate the reality of a situation one must get into the culture. Once pros and cons, needs and potential fulfillments, hungers and possible satisfactions come into clear view, then and only then can the guide articulate a vision for the future. The groundwork laid, vision casting takes shape for both leader and people. "Without a vision the people perish"; with a vision, spoken with excitement and imagination, people follow and help build the dream.

A theory of vision casting is one thing; doing it with originality and communicative skill is quite another. One man goes to an institution, discovers its unstable structure, and closes it. Not David McKenna. He dreams a dream big enough to find a way to rescue the organization and gets enthusiastic help doing it. Over and again, Dr. McKenna has sized up a situation in a church or college, looked at the options, and come up with a plan not merely to save a cause but to advance it. Just here lies one of the extraordinary gifts possessed by David L. McKenna. No wonder his denomination made him Churchman of the Year in 1990.

2) ***Optimism.*** When the situational reality is clearly defined, one will lead not with naïve hope, but realistic optimism. One clear way to do this is to publish the goals so the leader will be held accountable. If a goal could not be achieved, David always explained the failure to his people. To "cover" robs one of honesty and therefore of leadership. But actually hitting targets inspires people with optimism. Whether a leader sees aims achieved or not, one must continue to be optimistic and then remind oneself that to lose optimism is to lose leadership.

One of the "in" words today, *conflictable*, stands in stark contrast to another term, *constructable*. The pessimist looks at the conflicts, the optimist at the constructive. Habitually, creatively, winsomely, David McKenna sees the possibilities in any situation, and then eloquently communicates how to make something eminently constructive. He does not see merely surface potential, but speaks with solid research findings. That makes him a realistic optimist.

3) *Trust, not fear.* David works on the principle that as a leader he must earn trust every day. Administrators, always questioned because of their authority (who doesn't question authority figures?), must do exactly what they promised to do. Just there lies the secret of maintaining the trust line.

The result? Trust—not fear that the chief will shuffle the cards on you. Faith in the leader becomes the foundation for developing not only some winners, but for making most feel like achievers. Competition has its place, say, on the tennis court, but the work of the church is no mere game. David wants to create win-win situations wherever possible. And such a result! Committees, institutions, commissions have often brought projects to a higher level of fulfillment than thought possible.

4) *Strategic presence.* A leader cannot appear everywhere; he must choose where and when to go. The chair of a committee rarely requests the vice chair to preside; a seminary president always goes to faculty meetings; election to a commission requires attendance. And the family! A leader cannot afford to be an absentee husband and father, so David worked diligently at church attendance with his family. Yes, he had many invitations to do weekend preaching missions, but how much more strategic can one get than to identify with his family?

Part of strategic presence relates to the common touch. David loves eating with people. He dines right along with committee members, often invites colleagues out, and frequently has eaten with students in dining halls. At Asbury Seminary he ate with students at least once a week.

5) *Joy.* To do the will of God, says McKenna, brings joy as the natural by-product. This leadership principle he sees

as part of his theology of leadership. The biblical stories make clear not once or twice, but throughout the Scriptures, that when one does the will of God, He looks down on His children with great pleasure and gives witness to that reward. The bottom line: the secret of joy lies in obeying God's instructions.

When the chief brings to Kingdom labor a cheerful spirit, work is done faster and better, and people tend to catch enthusiasm for the task. Asbury Seminary is a pretty serious place, but David infused the atmosphere with joy and intellectual excitement. What a way to lead!

6) *Show appreciation.* The first and last task of the leader is to thank those who make achieving a goal possible. David knows how to build people up, to love them into the kingdom of accomplishment. He understands clearly that he cannot possibly do big tasks by himself. This accounts for his never-ending notes of appreciation and words of affirmation.

This, too, shows the way he constructed bridges and built rapport. He sent calendars for new mothers to seminary wives who had just given birth; he mailed candleholders to party hostesses; he gave students his books with personal inscriptions.

Churchman Mentors

"Spectacular achievements," says Roger Staubach, "are always preceded by unspectacular preparation." Mentoring, a quiet and often unheralded affair, rarely comes across as spectacular. Special people, of course, serve as mentors. David McKenna talks especially about persons who helped him grow into a leader. A representative list of persons randomly selected follows.

Martin Marty, professor of religion at the University of Chicago, appealed to David because of the famous theologian's fine mind. Marty, a walking encyclopedia of religious information, put people and movements into perspective. His analytical intellect could sort out data and synthesize it brilliantly. As often as possible, David profited from dialogue with this celebrated Lutheran clergyman.

Curry Mavis, Free Methodist pastor, college president, and professor, opened doors for David while in seminary. For example, he and David, long before clinical pastoral education, designed a hospital chaplaincy program, a practicum that David did to great profit. He learned much about human behavior and pastoral care from that experience.

E. A. Cutler, a district superintendent in Michigan at the time David attended college, spoke up for the young student and got him into pastoral ministry and ordained. That loving and fervent support helped launch David on a church vocation.

Robert Fine, pastor of Seattle First Church while David served as president of Seattle Pacific, brought to the pulpit the integration of intellect and Bible in a most captivating tone. David took notes on sermon after sermon and found himself advancing both spiritually and intellectually. Bob's death affected Dave profoundly. During Pastor Fine's last days in the hospital, President McKenna visited him. Afterward Dave said to his wife, Jan, voicing his grief, "Bob will never preach again." Bob and Dave had often breakfasted together and sensed kinship, both men profiting from one another's company.

Billy Graham told World Methodist Council general secretary Joe Hale, "I want to read every book David McKenna writes." David and Billy, longtime friends, enjoy and profit from one another's company. Often Graham receives gratis copies of McKenna's books.

Hugh White, a fervently dedicated lay churchman and executive, spotted David's talent early on. White, a Spring Arbor College board member, wanted to see David, fresh out of university, president of the college. He believed in him and gave him full support. Through the years, Hugh encouraged David, worked with him on boards and committees, and watched him develop into a productive church leader. David has never lost his admiration for Hugh White, creative and nonstop Kingdom builder. Hugh helped create the World Fellowship of the Free Methodist Church, opening doors to independent and expanded ministries in countries around the world.

James Gregory, a Canadian clergyman who settled in the United States, served to open David's mind to the grandeur of God and the possibilities of holy living. David watched the mature Gregory preach, teach, serve as college president, write, and edit. Great and creative minds have always fascinated David McKenna; intellectual horizons stretch him to exciting frontiers of knowledge and imaginative goal setting.

The Churchman Develops Churchmen

How do we take seriously the divine assignments to develop genuine Christian leaders? That question has taken a sizable chunk of David's time over the years.

The first step? Identify potential leaders. Such people, often students in high school or college, show unusual depth of concern about the church and demonstrate potential for intellectual growth. To spot such people constitutes the first step in leadership development.

The second step? Go after them! Cultivate, recruit, and give them a chance to try their wings. McKenna has an uncanny skill just here. He seems to sense where people can start and succeeds sufficiently to encourage them to pursue their gifts. Part of this ability came to formation in him because when he was young himself, leaders gave him opportunities. For example, Dr. Harold Kuhn, professor of philosophy at Asbury Theological Seminary when David studied there, would ask David to substitute teach when he had to be absent. Students of those days still talk about David's lectures.

Since steps one and two are the initial phases, mentoring now must express itself in a kind of covenant relationship marked by consistency, faithfulness, honest asking and personal disciplines and leadership skills. After a lifetime of diligent effort at finding and developing leaders, David has helped churches find pastors, denominations select executives, institutions locate CEOs, and Christian colleges and seminaries discover presidents, deans and faculty.

His secret lies not only in being able to spot talent, but also in painting an exciting picture colored with hope and opportunity. Sometimes according to his critics, he has painted the colors too brightly, and once in the job the idealism has not materialized. But those who have entered fully into Dr. McKenna's excitement have found fulfillment both in the process of becoming leaders and in their sense of Kingdom accomplishments.

The Gambling Story: A Case in Christian Leadership

While serving as president of Seattle Pacific, on one occasion David McKenna addressed the Governor's Prayer Breakfast at Olympia, state capital of Washington. Governor Dan Evans attended. Impressed with David, Dan confided his concern about the vote of the people in Washington State to allow gambling. Evans the conservative did not want that raging tiger to destroy the lives of innocent people, but the will of the people must be honored. Would David consider heading the Gambling Commission for the state?

David asked for two weeks to think, pray and get counsel. He went to see the publisher of the *Seattle Post Intelligencer* newspaper, who did not paint an inviting picture. David would suffer threats on his life and the lives of his family, and even if he succeeded in a measure, opponents would buy off the legislators, even the night before voting. President McKenna consulted with his college board, only to discover that they thought this an important Christian witness opportunity. David began to feel he must say yes to Governor Evans's request.

Actually, David was about to become part of a long line of Christian evangelical leaders battling social sins. Mark Matthews, years before, had pastored First Presbyterian, the largest Presbyterian church in the world, in the heart of Seattle. He had marched with believers right down the center of the red-light district, crying out against prostitution. Later in Seattle's history, Youth for Christ made its impact with Bob Pierce and others; Bob would later found World Vision. The Prayer Breakfasts, under the leadership of Abraham Veriede, started in Seattle with the express goal of cleaning up the city and state. Concerned citizens hammered at the gates of heaven for change. The upshot: a succession of Christian governors in the state and committed mayors in Seattle.

When David McKenna came to Seattle in 1968, he wanted to make his college a beacon light in the city. What could a Christian evangelical college do to transform the metropolis? President McKenna worked diligently at chapel addresses. He painted a picture of youth and faculty tackling the very crucible of the urban world. So when Dan Evans called from Olympia asking David to head a blue ribbon committee to study gambling, what alternative did he really have? He had to practice what he preached.

Governor Evans wanted a leader with conservative values, yet a person with scholarly habits to insure objectivity. David had a rough time coming to grips with this new challenge. In his boyhood home, the family did not even play a game of authors, for that, like poker, was a card game. Mom and Dad McKenna did not allow a hint of gambling. So when the college president saw an article in the *Seattle Post Intelligencer* about the activities of the Eastern Syndicate, he found himself highly motivated to fight wagering. The Syndicate, buying up wasteland along the Columbia River, was determined to install casinos.

The decision put motivation in gear. David and Dan talked, and the governor announced in a press conference that President McKenna would head the State Gambling Commission. The forming of the commission led to twenty-eight persons covering the full spectrum of belief, some conservative, some very liberal.

Soon the commission's chairperson realized he must educate himself. His discoveries did not paint a pleasant picture. Wherever gambling entered a society, every crime escalated, every species of gaming opened doors to cheating, police went corrupt. In a word, the power of money took precedence over morals. The pressure in the state legislature was staggering. Emotions, of course, ran high. Having learned to build his case on facts, David did his homework thoroughly. The Ford Foundation, he discovered, had done crucial research. Promises by advocates of gambling never came through; only token monies went to education, and almost nothing went to clean up a city. Atlantic City, a gambling center, stands as a monument to dead promises.

Hard-earned research and the challenge of conflict management brought good results. Major gambling interests like casinos and lotteries lost out, though bingo, raffles and sweepstakes got permission to function. Conservative Christians had mixed reactions, but if politics is the art of compromise, the consequences looked pretty good. Good indeed, for to the vast sweep of parasitic, nonproductive wagering and the financial bleeding of innocent families the state said a resounding "No!" The McKenna Report will go down in history as an example of genuine Christian leadership.

Yet legislators did not pay close attention to this clergyman president's oral report in the capitol at Olympia. However, *U.S. News & World Report* spelled out the story, and the lottery stayed away from the state of Washington for several years, actually not entering the state until McKenna came to Asbury Theological Seminary in 1982.

Winning over Criticism

Patch Adams and David McKenna, one in the medical profession, the other a member of the clergy, have both met severe criticism. The movie *Patch Adams* makes it ever so clear that Patch had a rough time even from medical school days. After all, how could one person penetrate the citadel of established health care and bring reform? But Patch worked at it. He established a medical center in West Virginia where the poor can come for help; thousands have benefited.

McKenna has, through the years, suffered a similar kind of criticism. Idealist? Oh yes, but do idealists really make a difference? A cynical seminarian sat in Asbury's chapel listening to David in his early years as president, laughing up his sleeve at "these big plans." Besides, how could the new president execute his elaborate design and at the same time romp around the globe in the interests of both the seminary and worldwide Methodism? Others quipped, "We don't see our president often. He's away more than he's here." Some wag even put up a sign that said, "Lost: David McKenna."

Patch has fun with his critics. He plows right through the criticism with humor, using clowning as one of his devices. David gets a big laugh out of the "Lost: David McKenna" signs. He does not allow the criticism to get to him. I once asked him if burnout threatened him. "What if you wake up in the night all worried?" I queried. Without missing a beat, he replied, "I would wake up laughing."

Nor does David McKenna go paralytic when a leadership effort goes awry. He had hoped to make a retreat center out of a southern mansion on the edge of Wilmore. The seminary had acquired it, and with the generous allotment of land and the possibilities of restructuring, it would make a most suitable place for conferences. That never happened. The property developed into the next president's home—and a very lovely one at that—but David, not crying over spilled milk, went right on to another project.

A seminary board member decried the fact that he had never entered President McKenna's home. Another critiqued him because of an almost habitual late arrival at meetings. One theory that emerged about his tardiness was that it served as a ploy to command attention. But David paid no attention to these critiques, though he smarted under them. He resolutely avoided exercises either in trivialities or in futility. He could have retorted with damaging words. "I don't have time for that," he once said after a dinner party.

That doesn't mean David could not get firm—sometimes with a look of the eyes, at other times a forthright statement defining the lines between right and wrong, or yet again a private word to clarify an issue. What did come across in the long haul was kindness. Always with a pastoral heart, he showed concern for people in their need. Writer Henry James made a poignant and simple statement that sums up David's intent in leading people: "Three things in human life are important: the first is to be kind. The second is to be kind. And the third is to be kind."

Accomplishments

Where does one begin? Where does one end? A director of the National Association of Evangelicals and many times a writer and speaker for that ecumenical group, Dr. McKenna has earned the respect of serious evangelicals across the nation and around the world. No wonder he was one of the founders of *Leadership* magazine, a writer for *Christianity Today*, and author of publication after publication dealing in part or in whole with leadership issues. In all this, Dr. McKenna has helped many a preacher, administrator and director because much of his published matter targets Christian church leadership. Yes, he writes for secular journals, but even there Christian leadership principles, always marked by integrity, shine through with clarity. McKenna's quick thinking and ability to summarize points and bring ideas to climax all distinguish him as a productive Christian leader.

But he sees his chief accomplishments in people. He believes in persons. He gives assignments to committee members or directors and then lets them exercise their own creativity in achieving goals. If they do not produce or if they go against agreed policy, he exercises discipline by firmly defining parameters. His ability to define tasks, then lead by suggestion, but seldom command, sets him apart as a leader of men and women and as a developer of leaders and followers.

The scope of his leadership comes into view a little more specifically with a recital of honors, a few listed here:

Outstanding Young Man of the Year, U.S. Junior Chamber of Commerce, 1965.

Outstanding Citizen, Municipal League of Seattle and King County, 1976.

Paul Harris Fellow, Rotary Club of Seattle, 1982.

Religious Heritage of America's 1993 Outstanding Educator.

National Association of Evangelicals' 1994 J. Elwin Wright Award for Advancing Evangelical Cooperation at National and International Levels.

Author of the Quadrennium, Light and Life Communications, Free Methodist Church, 1999.

Then scan McKenna's community and civic contributions:

Jackson Rotary Club, Jackson, Michigan, 1966-68.

President, United Way, Jackson, Michigan, 1967-1968.

Chair, Governor's Select Committee on Gambling, Washington State, 1973.

Chair, Community Research and Development Division, United Way of the Bluegrass, 1982-1990.

Vice President Bluegrass Tomorrow, Lexington, Kentucky, 1989-1992.

Trustee/Director:
Pacific Science Center, 1969-1982.
Seattle Rotary Club, 1972-1973.
United Way of King County, 1976-1978.
The Seattle Foundation, 1976-1982.
Seattle Chamber of Commerce, 1977-1982.
Washington Athletic Club, 1978-1982.
United Way of the Bluegrass, 1982-1994.

Wherever McKenna serves, the Christian witness goes with him, appropriately, socially skilled and without compromise. The more specifically religious associations call to mind a longer list, and denote his passion for the church of Jesus Christ. Look over these roles of McKenna the churchman:

Delegate to:
World Methodist Conference, London, 1966.
World Methodist Council, Nairobi, 1986.
International Congress on World Evangelization, Lausanne, 1974.
Consultation on World Evangelization, Bangkok, 1980.
Consultation on Theological Education, World Congress on Evangelization, Manila, 1989.
World Methodist Council Executive Committee, Jamaica, 1988 and Bulgaria, 1992.

Board of Reference:
Black Evangelistic Enterprise.
Ugandan Relief.
Youth for Christ International.
American Corporation of World Evangelical Fellowship.
Overseas Council.

Board of Directors:
National Association of Evangelicals (Executive Committee), 1976-1992.
Bread for the World, 1980-1986.
Executive Editor, *Religious Book Club Journal*, 1987-present.
Executive Committee, Religious Book Club, Crossroads/Continuum Publishing Company, 1988-present.

Officer:
Vice President of the North American Section of the World
    Methodist Council and a member of the World Executive
    Committee.

Advisory Boards:
Ministers' Personal Library.
Leadership Journal.
Guideposts Home Bible Study Program.
Peace, Freedom and Security Studies Program (National Asso-
    ciation of Evangelicals).
Azusa Pacific University, President's Council, Haggard School
    of Theology, 1999-present.

Praise God for a leader like David McKenna, tireless, creative, willing to serve! Asked how he could achieve so much, he half turns aside, a bit embarrassed at the recital of accomplishments, and answers, "Grace. God's grace."

THE EDUCATOR
Apostle to Higher Education

'Tis education forms the common mind.
Just as the twig is bent, the tree's inclined.
—Alexander Pope

THE EDUCATOR:
Apostle to Higher Education

Donald English, late president of the British Methodist Church and a friend of Asbury Theological Seminary, tells a story about the Lewis chain of department stores—a megacorporation. In Birmingham, England,
the Lewis store wanted to enlarge, which required buying an
adjoining Quaker meetinghouse. The Lewis directors wrote
to the Friends Society:

> "Dear Sirs: We wish to expand our property. Your little meet-
> inghouse is in the way, and we are willing to pay whatever
> price you want so that we may demolish your building and
> expand.
>
> Yours faithfully,
The Lewis Company."

The directors received this reply:

> "Dear Sirs: We notice the intention of the Lewis Company to
> expand and your willingness to buy our building, but we
> wish you respectfully to know that we are determined to
> stay where we are. If it would help, we are willing to buy
> the Lewis Company at any price you name.
>
> Faithful in the service of our Lord Jesus Christ, Cadbury."

Dr. English, in telling this story, underscored our human
tendency to think that places like the Friends meetinghouse
look pretty small against the "big guys" who will surely win
the battle. But English noted that the size of the building did
not determine the winner. The Cadbury family (and a much
larger corporation) identified with the Quakers, and the wee
meetinghouse where the Cadburys worshiped would under
no circumstances yield to the department store chain. Who

signed the letter settled the matter. God's signature has been on David McKenna's life, and that has settled the matter.

Modest Beginnings

In 1953 David went to Spring Arbor College to work in both the high school and junior college. In those days, junior colleges often had a high school program. David taught, served as dean, and then became principal. He did all this while carrying a full academic load at the University of Michigan, Ann Arbor, where he eventually earned both the master's degree and a Ph.D. in higher education. In 1959 he became vice president of Spring Arbor College.

With a new doctor of philosophy degree, however, David went to work at Ohio State University, directing the Center for Higher Education. After only a brief time in Ohio, he returned to his alma mater to work for his mentor, Algo Henderson, director of higher education at the University of Michigan. Algo was a skeptic, yet the two men worked well together. In fact, they developed a national prototype for advanced academic work in higher education. To this day men and women enter the University of Michigan to earn graduate degrees under this model.

Thinking he had firmly settled into a prestigious job, David nonetheless received a surprise call from Spring Arbor College to serve as president. A personal struggle ensued; much prayer with agony of soul characterized the days of decision. Finally, David knew he must talk to Algo. The moment of confrontation came. Would Algo, the unbeliever, chastise him? David drove to the university, left his wife and baby in the car on a campus parking lot, and walked with trepidation to Dr. Henderson's office.

Much to David's amazement, Henderson said, "If Spring Arbor College is what you have trained for, go!" A relieved young man left the campus, excited over the prospects of heading a small Christian college.

Little did he know at the time, however, what an inconvenience he had created for his University of Michigan boss. His wife, David learned later, had just received news of a cancer diagnosis. More, Algo Henderson would have to postpone a sabbatical to do the work David would have done.

What had David McKenna really decided? Had he forfeited a first-class position to serve a tiny junior college? Surely he had slipped a cog. What would his friends say? Then David recalled his full surrender to God during his seminary days. "Not my will, Lord, but yours," he had prayed. Suddenly that petition came to memory with the fire of God's blessing. He did know, after all, that he had made the right decision.

A Young President

Elected to the top post at Spring Arbor College at age thirty, he took office a month after his thirty-first birthday, the youngest college president in America. David wasted no time. He envisioned a fully accredited four-year college. He got on the phone with Tom Jones, president of Earlham College in Indiana. Tom responded warmly to David and became a mentor. In fact, the relationship with Jones resulted in a defining moment for the young president and his college career. Jones asked a pivotal question: "What's the big idea behind Spring Arbor College?" President Jones himself had had to answer that question for Earlham. To respond specifically to that question would define the school.

David proceeded to produce well-documented, carefully reasoned "concept" monographs in which he itemized the problems of the small Christian college and indicated the way to meet those challenges. The meat of the pamphlets became so well known that McKenna surfaced as a progressive leader in the small Christian college scene across America. For his own college, President McKenna projected the "Spring Arbor Concept" to faculty, students and the Spring

Arbor constituency. To this day the Spring Arbor College faculty talks about the "Spring Arbor Concept," and everyone knows it as an integrated higher-education experience in a Christ-oriented context.

In summary, the reason for a Christian evangelical college, according to McKenna, can be expressed in just six words: "The integration of faith and learning." That formula captured the imagination of faculty, students, constituents and the accreditation people too. And before Spring Arbor College ever graduated a single senior, the unheard-of came to pass—accreditation! It could never happen in just the same way in today's academic world.

The Making of a President

During these early Spring Arbor, Michigan, years, David leaned heavily on his intellectual understanding of higher education administration, having earned a doctorate in the field. But no matter how much head knowledge one possesses, nothing takes the place of experience, hard-earned and character-building.

One day President McKenna read a statement by David Rockefeller, who noted that a leader must "see the vision, state the mission, and set the tone" for his or her organization. With the insight this triad brought, McKenna now moved to a new level of academic leadership and development. That triad is really the essence of his book *Power to Follow, Grace to Lead*. Vision, mission and tone would color his academic leadership for the rest of his career.

Lewis Mayhew, a Stanford University professor, brought to light David's joyous tone in leadership. The autobiographical foreword of this book tells that story. What should be added here is that the universal mark of authentic New Testament religion is none other than joy, the delight God's Spirit-filled servants have in doing His will. Literally thousands of students have seen and felt the cheer of

President McKenna. That relates significantly to Christian witness.

Still another step in the formation of McKenna's presidential character came with the reading of Max DuPree's book *Leadership Is an Art.* In that volume DuPree said, "The first responsibility of a leader is to define reality. The last responsibility of a leader is to say 'Thank you.' In between the two, the leader must be a debtor and a servant." President McKenna took that guidance seriously. He learned to define reality, developed the gift of saying thank you, and confesses, "I am still learning what it means to be a debtor and a servant."

David's son Doug researched leadership characteristics in chief executive officers. As part of Doug's graduate studies, he studied the qualities developed by top-drawer leaders. He learned that this level of managers had begun to learn the skills in their twenties. Doug examined the starting and restarting of organizations, hiring and firing, assuming responsibility for budgets—the whole nine yards. Researching his dad, too, he found his father possessed the qualities of outstanding leadership and had pretty well learned them in his twenties. Doug McKenna concluded that God uniquely prepared his father for presidential administration even during the time he worked on his graduate degree in higher education at Ann Arbor.

Commenting on all of this, David asks, "Isn't that another example of prevenient grace at work? God still moves in mysterious ways."

Joy in Crises

Never an easy row to hoe, the presidency brought challenges, sometimes daily. One college president commented, "On average I meet two or three crises a day." David identifies fully with that comment and considers the assessment to be realistic. At Spring Arbor, for example, accreditation did not come easily. Thinking he had help in place to take the college through the accreditation process, McKenna watched his neatly put-together system crumble before his eyes. Much to his shock, he discovered a lack of integrity in one of the leaders and had to take charge of the procedure himself. But he refused to collapse under the new load; with joy, laughter and hard work he plodded on to victory.

At Seattle Pacific he met a similar challenge, this time with finance. Getting a phone call from the bank, he learned that the college's line of credit had stopped dead in its tracks. Because that fact was unknown to virtually everyone in the school's administration, the news came as a shock. David suddenly had to learn about a new world, the world of high finance, and with optimism and enthusiasm he went to the public to raise money, and cleared the matter in the remarkably short time of four years.

On still another occasion, the editor and student reporters of the Seattle Pacific student paper, the *Falcon*, took liberties that pushed their journalism out of bounds. The president had to teach young authors responsibility with their pens. McKenna shut down the paper; the students learned. Mentors rejoiced.

Fortunately, in the providence of God, happy events come in a never-ending line to counterbalance the crises. The Seattle Pacific students decided, for example, to make their president "King for a Day." They made a throne colored in gold and bright hues, put a monarch's robe on him and a crown on his head. He sat high on the steps of McKinley Auditorium, participating fully, much to the delight of students.

The joyous events, too numerous to mention in detail, include a surprise birthday party with seminary faculty for the president's wife, Janet, and dinner meetings with friends and well-known people like Senator Mark Hatfield, anthropologist Margaret Mead, and world political figure Charles Malik. They also include meetings in Washington, D.C., to assist in advising the president of the United States. The list goes on; enough to say that McKenna's gift of joy comes as the direct result of God's grace. It does not leave in crises, but expresses itself in the peaceful undertow of his soul through the challenges and surprising delights of service.

Developing Faculty

"An institution of higher learning is only as strong as its faculty," says President McKenna with unmistakable conviction. Accordingly, he has given a good share of his energy to choosing and grooming promising young people for teaching positions. So intently has he given himself to this enterprise that he formed a philosophy for faculty development. It begins with identification. He never fails to look for potential classroom leaders. He likes to find them when they are young and encourages them to go on for higher degrees. That is all part of what he calls "cultivating talented people."

An academic administrator must recruit talent. Traditionally, universities have attracted gifted people, sometimes because of higher salaries. But McKenna has developed remarkable powers of persuasion, showing the romance and influence of Christian evangelical higher education. He has recruited dozens of faculty.

How does the administration develop young scholars into mature teaching faculty? Not an easy challenge. The first step: recognize that young professionals, fresh out of graduate school, come to a campus position from a narrow and deep study context. They have specialized in a specific discipline and researched a single problem. Helping them see the larger picture of integrated learning defines an initial task of the administrative mentor. Socializing helps, and often informal experiences do a good job. Showing patience as the new teacher learns to cope with immature students wrestling to find their way also assists professors in relating to the real world. As time moves along, sabbaticals, research projects (sometimes assigned by the administration), and groups for cross-disciplinary stimulation and intellectual growth spur the maturation process.

Promotion, David believed, plays a significant role in personal and professional development. He took vigorous interest in helping faculty go on for higher degrees and often created funding. Years of service, too, factored into moving from instructor to assistant professor, then on to associate and full professorship, with salary increases at every new step.

In all this, David made clear that he entered a covenant relationship with his faculty. He had no intention of playing games, or merely doing things that just looked good. He bonded with his faculties in the grand enterprise of professional growth. He believed personal modeling played a significant role. He himself must live the characteristics of a growing teacher: reading, evaluation, analysis, public speaking, appearance, publication, and moral integrity—anything and everything that spelled mature leadership.

Evaluations must enter the picture of any progressive program. Student evaluations, written and specific, play their part. McKenna himself called for written evaluation of his presidential leadership and studied what he saw on the surveys. The biggest room, he believes, is the room for improvement. Often personal or committee interviews assisted in evaluating faculty personnel.

Another factor relates to the personal problems of his employees. Here is a faculty member who is connecting poorly with students, but the president discovers her home life is in shambles. There is a promising department director who does not perform up to par; the president learns in private interview that his sibling suffers a terminal disease. Another employee fights administration policy, but the president discovers unbelievably wretched childhood conditionings. Sensitive administrators must work with people in distress. The hurting, so preoccupied with personal problems they cannot handle reprimand, need affirmation and a listening ear. Who better to help them than the boss? Administrators stand in an opportune place to provide a special kind of therapy that can indeed mean personal growth and professional advancement.

Helping Other Institutions

David McKenna never went after teachers and administrators from a professionally selfish perspective. Always on the lookout for people who could serve anywhere, he often made recommendations to a whole spectrum of evangelical colleges and universities. In fact, he has assisted in picking some nine presidents, all happy choices.

However, he readily confesses, "I have not chosen winners every time." He listed half a dozen people he had recommended whose gifts had not found their proper home. David does not claim infallibility, but even in retirement, he continues, to do what he can to find and promote talent for Christian evangelical higher education.

Apostle to Higher Education

David has dedicated over four decades of service to the world of Christian higher education. He is in fact an apostle to higher education, a sent one, a pioneer to do breakthrough work.

He saw Spring Arbor College move from junior college status to a fully accredited four-year institution. He developed well-qualified, competent faculty to teach at the senior college level. He gave oversight to the construction of facilities to encourage the best teaching; for example, a forum in a central building, the very structure helping to create an atmosphere conducive to academic questioning and dialogue. An active radio station on campus became a laboratory for learning communications. A beautiful student center helped implement informal teaching and the development of social graces.

Going to Seattle Pacific College, David immediately dreamed of institutional witness in the heart of the city. He did a series of addresses in chapel highlighting the potential of students and faculty to bring Christ and resultant social change to Seattle. He modeled what he preached; this explains his active life in the university communities—Seattle University and University of Washington—and his involvement in civic organizations such as Rotary, in which he made a name for himself as a public speaker.

David also worked arduously at putting his integration-of-faith-and-learning concept into the curriculum of Seattle Pacific. He gave a series of chapel talks on "A Vision of Wholeness," in which he focused on his curricular dream. The chapel, he believed, was the "President's Course" for the whole school, a classical pattern he learned from Elton Trueblood. The result: an enriched and more integrated curriculum that helps students learn how the gospel articulates with, and must infuse, every facet of life and work.

David had a still bigger dream: to make of the college a full-fledged university. He sensed that the faculty needed heightened self-esteem; moving up to the status of a university suggested one way to get at that. University status would also spread and enhance the institution's Christian witness. Today Seattle Pacific University enjoys enrollments into the thousands and a faculty into the hundreds.

At Asbury Theological Seminary, David worked on developing a world-class theological institution. Today many see Asbury as the world's chief Wesleyan school of graduate theology. After arriving on campus, McKenna soon learned to move in the seminary world, becoming an officer and speaker at meetings of the seminary presidents organization, and holding offices in the World Methodist Council. He continued Dr. McPheeters's acquaintance with the Beeson family, developing a relationship also with Colonel Bill Conger, executor of the Ralph W. Beeson estate.

Bill and Dave determined to redo the entire campus; today there is a magnificent quad with new buildings, including Beeson Manor guest house, McKenna Chapel named for David and Janet McKenna, the Beeson Center which houses the Beeson Pastors' classrooms and study cubicles along with seminar rooms and preaching chapels, and a state-of-the-art media center. In addition, the student center received a major expansion and refurbishing. A fountain lighted by night and a life-sized statue of John Wesley grace the interior of the quad. More significantly than physical facilities, of course, is the first-class faculty that has been assembled—teachers, writers, conference leaders, many known internationally.

A summary glance at the career of David L. McKenna, apostle to higher education, looks like this:

> Instructor in Psychology, Dean of Men, Academic Dean, Vice President, Spring Arbor College, 1953-1960.
>
> Lecturer in Higher Education, University of Michigan, 1958-1960.
>
> Assistant Professor and Coordinator for Higher Education, Ohio State University, 1960-1961.
>
> President, Spring Arbor College, 1961-1968.
>
> President, Seattle Pacific University, 1968-1982.
>
> President, Asbury Theological Seminary, 1982-1994.

Recognition

McKenna has addressed literally countless college communities and written scores of articles in educational journals and professional and lay magazines on responsible evangelical higher education. He has contributed his philosophy of education to many published anthologies, sat on boards, and spent hours on the telephone. In a word, he has given himself unselfishly to the cause of genuine learning in a Christian context.

No wonder recognitions—honors, awards, degrees—have come to this dedicated apostle. A list of the colleges awarding him honorary doctoral degrees is representative of the appreciation of a wide circle of admirers:

Greenville College, 1970.

Houghton College, 1974.

Spring Arbor College, 1976.

Lewis and Clark College, 1978.

Seattle University, 1982.

Marion College, 1983.

Roberts Wesleyan College, 1986.

Asbury College, 1994.

Trinity Western University, 2000.

McKenna appreciates these honorary degrees, but talks little about them. What captures his attention is the hard work of advancing education. A sample of his wide recognition and leadership in the academic world, beyond but complementing his presidential career, looks like this:

Chair, Michigan Commission of College Accreditation, 1961-1963.

Director, Association of Michigan Independent Colleges, and Universities, 1961-1968.

Founding Chairman, Christian College Consortium, 1970-1982, and Member of National Advisory Board, 1982-present.

Co-Chair, Independent Colleges of Washington, 1968-1970 and 1979-1981, Director, 1968-1982.

Chair, Independent Friends of Higher Education, 1969-1974, Director, 1968-1982.

Member, Spring Arbor College (now University) Board of Trustees, 1983-present.

Member, Washington State Council for Postsecondary Education, 1969-1974.

Member, Inter-association President's Committee on Accreditation, American Council on Education, 1979-1980.

Commissioner, Northwest Association of Schools and Colleges, 1975-1979.

Director, National Association of Independent Colleges and Universities, 1976-1980; Secretary, 1978.

Director, Council on Postsecondary Accreditation, 1979-1981.

Member, Advisory Committee on Theological Education Management, Association of Theological Schools, 1986-1994.

Chair, Task Force on Long-range Planning for Organization, Structure and Staffing, Association of Theological Schools, 1988-1994.

Member, Advisory Committee on Theological School Trustee Leadership Program, Association of Governing Boards, 1987-1994.

President, Fellowship of Evangelical Seminary Presidents, 1993-1994.

Chair, Board of Trustees, Spring Arbor College, 1998-1999.

The Rest of the Story

We began this chapter with the story told by Donald English. He finishes his narrative with this to-the-point comment: "We may look at the world and feel greatly overwhelmed . . . but the thing to be remembered is that it is the Lord who signs the letters!" Just there lies the apostolic success of David McKenna in taking struggling institutions and bringing them to remarkable levels of productivity.

THE FATHER
Primary Priority

A man ought to live so that everybody knows he is a
Christian . . . and most of all, his *family* ought to know.
—D. L. Moody

THE FATHER:
Primary Priority

David McKenna loves his family deeply. It all began in his boyhood home. His dad always appeared at his son's big public moments: the oratory contests, the debating events, the concerts. In the back of the auditorium, there sat his dad. "Dad always showed up," David underscores as he reminisces, "but I don't know how he did it. And I cannot be too grateful."

That set the stage for David's own father role. On a special occasion he hurried back from an appointment to shoot baskets with his son Doug at the family home in Spring Arbor. Before moving from Spring Arbor to Seattle, he felt he must consult Doug. What about leaving his schoolmates who admired him for his involvement in sports and for his high grades? Would Doug really want to make the move? Doug thought the change would present a great challenge and provide fresh excitement. As it turned out, Doug became an All-American soccer player, graduated from Seattle Pacific, and went on to do a Ph.D. But David had been willing to leave the presidency of Spring Arbor College for the Seattle job only if his oldest child felt comfortable with the move.

Not all the children were excited about the move, however. Suzanne went along with the change, but secretively the second grader did not want to leave all of her friends. She knew she would especially miss her best friend, Kendra, and her first boyfriend, Marcelle. Years later, Kendra became her roommate at SPU, and Marcelle went there, too. Suzanne graduated with a bachelor of arts in Fine Arts and is now Senior Recruiter for Marketing at Microsoft.

When David considered transferring from Seattle to

Wilmore, all the children were out of the nest except Rob. Would Rob feel right about leaving the familiar surroundings of a great city and resettling in a small town in central Kentucky? Rob thought relocating a good idea, provided this was God's will. The teenager got into sports in his Kentucky high school, went on to college, and later earned a doctorate. He now teaches at Seattle Pacific University.

On the day the seminary board of trustees elected David McKenna to the presidency, he got a forthright call from one of the trustees saying David had no right to become president because of his denominational affiliation. How could Asbury even entertain the idea of a non-United Methodist as president? David tried to persuade his attacker to "wait and see," but to no avail. What a depressing moment! But David's mood would change, and it happened in a most delightful way.

On the night of the nasty phone call, David received another call, this one from J. C. McPheeters, president emeritus of Asbury Theological Seminary. David could not return the call until eight o'clock the next morning, when he dialed Operator 6, who connected him with Dr. McPheeters at Redwood Camp in northern California. With Operator 6 still on the line, dear old Dr. McPheeters began shouting, "This is the day the Lord has made, let us rejoice and be glad in it!" The operator, terribly amused, totally forgot to ask him if he would accept the charges. And even before David McKenna could identify himself, J. C. said in his booming voice, "David, I have just been praying for you, Janet, Douglas, Debra, Sue, and Robbie. By the way, do you water-ski?" David said that yes, his family loved waterskiing. "Great," Dr. Mac replied. "As soon as you get to the seminary I want you to take a little time to drive to my cabin at Dale Hollow, Tennessee, so that Robbie can water-ski."

David cherishes that call about as much as any telephone conversation he ever had. He cannot quit talking and writing about it, because, as he says, "I was totally overwhelmed by the fact that Dr. McPheeters knew every member of my family by name and sensed that Rob was the tag-along for whom the move would be most difficult." David added, "There could never be doubt that he was a great man of prayer with a gifted sensitivity to the mind of the Holy Spirit. What a legacy!"

David declares, "My family is my greatest joy," and then goes on to say that June 2000 marks fifty years of marriage for him and Janet. He says more: "All my children belong to Jesus Christ, all have strong marriages, and I have ten grandkids." Of the marriages, he speaks with pride that he presided at each of the four weddings, all of which took place at First Free Methodist Church, Seattle. With evident conviction in voice and expression he says, "My family is my first priority."

The Delight of Small Children

One day in the lobby of the Free Methodist church in Wilmore, Florence Mannoia told a thoroughly delightful tale of something that had happened over four decades ago in Spring Arbor, Michigan. While both fathers worked at the college, the Mannoia and McKenna children grew up together, sharing yards as a play area. Jan McKenna and Florence Mannoia lived next door to each other in Harmony Lane, which they dubbed "Mortgage Lane." Both mothers taught school and commuted some 120 miles round trip to finish their education.

The children of these two busy mothers staged a wedding. It turned out, as Florence said, "just a little less than elegant." It all took place in the Mannoia garage, cleaned and swept by a half dozen neighbor kids. The lovely Debbie McKenna and the handsome Kevin Mannoia, both under five years of age, would say their vows. Rehearsals went on for quite some days. Florence tells the rest of the story in her own words:

"Rehearsals for this spectacular went on for two weeks. The attention span of an already unwilling groom expired after the first half day. I learned later that they had bribed Kevin to continue practicing with everything their piggy banks could afford. Apparently, three days before the wedding date, the groom just plain threw in the towel, called it quits; that's it—no more!

"Now this gang never called in the parents until all else had failed. A brief consultation brought the conclusion that 'the wedding must go on.' While the groom found 'better' things to do, they pooled their resources and came up with five cents, which bought a Hershey bar. The young groom could have this chocolate bar if he would continue practicing. He took the bar, sat down on the back steps, and, before a drooling wedding party, including his bride-to-be, he ate the whole thing. I inquired about what was going on and was told of the offer that Kevin couldn't resist. After savoring every bite, he carefully licked all ten fingers. I went back to my work confident that the neighborhood project would go on.

"My peace of mind was short-lived. Suddenly 'Sergeant' Jimmy Mannoia, flanked by a platoon, including the bride's brother, Doug, landed flat-footed in my kitchen. With hand on hip, Sergeant announced, 'Kevin ate the whole Hershey bar and now he won't practice!' This was critical. This gang had called in the emergency squad and I was it. Sweet little Debbie McKenna stood by wide-eyed with disillusionment: What kind of man was she marrying? Kevin got my five-year-olds lecture on ethics and was finally persuaded that he had a moral obligation to continue playing their game; at least a candy bar's worth. For his chocolate, he must pay the fiddler.

"Saturday dawned, sunny and beautiful. Early in the afternoon I saw the neighborhood mothers, and Debbie's grandmother, headed toward our garage, decked out in hats and white gloves. I quickly changed into an afternoon dress and dashed out to join them, but only after I turned on pre-selected records on our stereo—extra loud—so the music might be heard by all in the garage. After all, this was the wedding music!

"The ten-year-old minister, Rick, solemnly addressed the groom, 'Kevin, do you take this bewedded woman to be your wife?' Debbie was a dream draped in her mother's old curtain, and Kevin muttered, 'I do.' Young Ricky's voice intoned, 'Debbie McKenna, do you take this bewedded man to be your husband?' There was more truth than met the ear in that question because Kevin's former bride, Linda, was seated with the guests. Demure little Debbie said, 'I do.' 'I pronounce you husband and wife,' the preacher said. To this day, I don't know if that darling bride was kissed because I had to dash for the Kool-Aid and chocolate chip cookies for the 'reception.' The whole affair ended by throwing rice all over the garage and driveway, which the little people later volunteered to sweep."

Reflecting on this delightful slice of memory, one cannot help but observe that in adult life Kevin became a bishop, Debbie a lawyer, and Jimmy a college president.

Family Modeling

Students love David McKenna for many reasons: his fine mind, his classy manner, his articulate speech, his gift of integration. But no reason stands out more vividly than his love of family. When he hears of an addition to a student family, he must tell Janet about the new baby, and runs to the nearest phone. And to all the new infants born during his presidency at Asbury Theological Seminary, he sent a copy of Kathleen Demaray's Calendar for New Mothers with paintings by Frances Hook.

One day in seminary chapel, President McKenna surprised Janet. Normally she busied herself with home concerns at 10 A.M., but that day her husband found a way to get her to chapel. With evident delight written on his face, David announced that he would soon fulfill one of his wife's fond dreams. She had always wanted "Breakfast at Tiffany's" in New Orleans. Well, he had purchased air tickets, and she would have her wish, breakfasting at the renowned restaurant. This announcement, much to the delight of the wonder-eyed seminarians, telegraphed a happy marriage.

That event, typical of David's surprises for his lovely wife, symbolizes their love for each other. He bought her a baby grand piano in the California blond finish that was her special color. He put on a surprise birthday party for her in the seminary's presidential home, complete with a cake with *Happy Birthday, Janet* written on it. He simply cannot stop lavishing love on Janet—dinners and lunches, packages and cards, phone calls and drives in the country. David adores Janet.

Coping with Disappointment

Shock invaded David's busy administrative life at Spring Arbor College when he received word that his dad would divorce his mother and marry Pauline. David had no idea such miserable news would confront him. He tried to reason with his father, but to no avail.

"Dad, what about your years in the church?"

"All a sham," he replied tersely.

"But your experience of Christ?"

"He means nothing to me."

David, caught in a paralytic moment, could say nothing. He stood stunned. That began a multi-year estrangement lasting from 1961 to 1973, and it had ramifications.

When Doug married, Grandpa McKenna wanted to come to the wedding. But Pauline would have created awkwardness for David's mother, then not in good health. So David had to say no to his father's request, thus protecting his mother's health. After all, Helen had lived a difficult life, working in a laundry after her husband left her, then laboring in a café to support herself. Clearly, David must relate sensitively to his mother, now old and ill.

By the time David's daughter Sue married, Helen had gone to heaven, and David wanted very much for his father to attend the wedding. David and his dad had been working at mending their relationship. He called his dad, who jumped with delight at the thought of going. But he never came. A week after the invitation, Dad McKenna suffered a stroke and became totally unresponsive. David flew to his father's bedside in Florida. A proud man, "Mac" always presented himself tidy and neat, but the stroke had prevented him from taking care of his beard. David shaved his father, knowing he would want to look good even in a comatose state.

Dad McKenna had become an Episcopalian, and when the priest came to call at the hospital, he comforted David with a beautiful sentence, "When your father could not sleep, he did not count sheep, he talked to the Shepherd." The pastor made the same statement in the funeral sermon, and David lives in the hope that his father had indeed returned to Christ as His Savior.

Waiting through the night in Chicago's O'Hare Airport for a delayed flight so he could get to his father's bedside, David miraculously found the McKenna Psalm, Psalm 121. Verse 8 especially comforted the weary traveler: "The LORD shall preserve thy going out and thy coming in from this time forth, and even for evermore" (KJV). When David arrived at the hospital, he posted Psalm 121 over his father's bed.

> I will lift up mine eyes unto the hills,
>   from whence cometh my help.
> My help cometh from the LORD,
>   which made heaven and earth.
> He will not suffer thy foot to be moved:
>   he that keepeth thee will not slumber.

Behold, he that keepeth Israel shall neither slumber nor sleep.
The LORD is thy keeper:
The LORD is thy shade upon thy right hand.
The sun shall not smite thee by day,
nor the moon by night.
The LORD shall preserve thee from all evil:
he shall preserve thy soul.
The LORD shall preserve thy going out and thy coming in
from this time forth, and even for evermore.

The Children Speak

One sees the proof of the pudding for parenting in the family members. I asked David's four children to write briefly about their father. What they say reveals their hearts:

Doug: "If my dad were a photographer, all his pictures would have crisp focus, rich depth of field, and bright, joyful colors. Through good times and bad, Dad has amazed me with his ability to maintain a crystal-clear focus on who he is, what he cares about and where he is going.

"As an educator, his focus has always been on students. He and Mom loved living in Hillford House at Seattle Pacific University mostly because they were smack in the middle of 3000 college students. While cars, stereos, and a constant stream of young people passing our windows would have driven most people crazy, it was a beehive of love and life for Mom and Dad. The 'Vision of Wholeness' was real at Seattle Pacific because it was practiced every moment of every day by a president who lived and worked alongside the students. Being whisked away to Herfy's at midnight for cheeseburgers, teaching classes in the School of Religion, traveling with the basketball team to regionals in Colorado, meeting one-on-one with a homesick freshman, cutting ivy at commencement—all were part of Dad's vision for 'his' students: that every one would have the opportunity to meet Jesus and have their lives turned inside out and upside down by His love during their time at Spring Arbor, Seattle Pacific, or Asbury.

"In over fifty years together, my mom and dad's focus on their love for each other has become sharper and sharper. Dad has reminded me many times that the best thing I can do for my kids is to love their mom. He really didn't need to remind me with words. Watching him be with Mom drove the message so deep in my bones that I know almost immediately when I think or act in ways that fail to put Diane—my wife—first. In their love for each other, Mom and Dad have given us a rare, priceless gift—a picture of a marriage in full bloom after fifty years of faith, love, work, patience and joy.

"If being a preacher's kid is tough, imagine being a president's and a preacher's kid at the same time. Sure there were expectations that created pressure to be someone other than myself, but over time I've learned that most of these expectations were not coming from Mom and Dad but from me. My dad's focus as a father is as crisp and singular as his focus as an educator or husband. My dad loves me, I know for sure, because every day of my life he has told me so—racing home from business trips to catch every game I played from the time I was six until I graduated from college, taking me to 'lunch' when I'd asserted my independence in irresponsible ways, calling to ask how things were going when my own kids had gone through hard times, listening to me when I said it was time to go to the hospital for his triple bypass, and always, always praying for me.

"My dad is not God, though when I was little I couldn't imagine that God could be any better than Dad. God never came home every day early enough to play catch with me when I was six. But over time, I've learned that Dad is human. Nevertheless, he's a very special human. That's because every day he turns himself over to Jesus and enthusiastically asks,

'What's next?' He looks to the hills for strength and then steps into the day-to-day fray with a spirit and vitality that can only come from the fact that he can hear all of creation singing to the Lord. I love my dad and my mom. I am completely mystified, yet undyingly thankful that God gave them to me."

Debra: "As a college president, my father had the reputation of being an exceptional visionary. He believed that, in order for a college to be a viable force in our society, it needed a national reputation and world exposure. As I look back to my childhood, I realize that Dad had vision for his children too.

"Long before airline travel became as easy as hopping on a city bus, my dad found a way to give us, his family, a world view. I grew up in the very beautiful small Michigan town of Spring Arbor where my dad was the president of Spring Arbor College. It was a magical childhood. My grandparents lived within a mile, my school was just across the street, and my friendships were numerous. It would have been easy to be contented with a sheltered and safe life, but not when your dad is David McKenna.

"The McKenna family became road warriors. With Dad at the wheel, logging at least five hundred miles per day, and Mom in the front seat begging him to stop for meals for us three small children, we traveled the country. By age ten, I had been to Niagara Falls; Cape Cod; New York City; Fort Lauderdale; Miami Beach; Chicago; the Grand Canyon; Laguna Beach, California; Mexico; Yosemite; and Yellowstone National Park. We visited Gettysburg one spring, Chicago for the winter Christmas lights, New York for the World's Fair, and Fort Lauderdale during college spring break. We climbed into the torch of the Statue of Liberty, rode a cable car in San Francisco, chased a bear from our garbage at Yellowstone, visited Disneyland, bartered in Tijuana and saw two Sea Worlds.

"I don't know how many miles Dad put on his cars, or the number of Holiday Inns he booked; but I do remember stopping at every historical land marker (and usually complaining about it), posing for more pictures than I can count, watching anxiously for the hotel sign because then we could eat and take a swim, begging to stop at a rest area ('just a few more miles, honey') and sweating through the desert heat in a car with no air conditioning. Through it all, Dad was indefatigable and, therefore, has given me the richest, most wonderful memories. He also gave me a love of our country that I carry with me to this day. And guess what? When my family travels from Michigan to Wyoming to ski during spring break—we drive."

Suzanne: "I was surprised a few years back to hear my dad say, 'If I had my life to live over again the only thing I would do differently would have been to have had more children.' I am so proud to be one of his children.

"I've learned the art of storytelling from my dad. For example, he recounts on my birthday, how on the afternoon I was born, he stood outside the hospital nursery window, waiting in anticipation. Then the big moment! A beautiful dark-headed infant, his own baby daughter. His heart beat with joy . . . in the meantime, my brother and sister headed off to the Ohio State football game.

"I learned early what it meant to follow the will of God when at age seven, our family moved from Spring Arbor, Michigan, to Seattle, Washington. My dad made decisions then and still does with the unanimous consent of the family and a promise from God in Psalm 121, which we call the 'McKenna Psalm.'

"I learned to accept defeat with grace when I didn't make the high school cheerleading squad. My dad was there to pick up the pieces, whisk my best friend and me off to a great restaurant where we laughed, told stories—but never one word was mentioned of my defeat. He always makes me feel special and loved.

"I learned at twenty of my dad's incredible faith when my future husband, Scott, walked into the president's office to ask Dad for my hand in marriage. Eighteen years of marriage later we know it took tremendous faith in God for my dad to let his 'little girl' go.

"Most of all I have learned that my dad's love of God and his family has given me a foundation of strength, faith and love that I will carry on with my family. I am so proud to be his daughter."

Robert: "My dad has always been my greatest hero. To me, he is a loving father, a professional mentor and one of my best friends. I have seen him put his God and family above all else, genuinely agonize over executive decisions that would impact the people and organizations he led, and take the time to relax and enjoy the things in life that give him peace. He is simply a very real kind of guy with deeply rooted convictions about the important things in life.

"As a father, my dad is always a loving and consistent presence. I can still see him standing on the sidelines of all my Little League soccer games in blowing wind and rain. He may never fully understand the impact of that image on me, but he certainly understands the importance of his presence at those events. I can also remember how upset I was when I backed out of our garage with my car door open, practically tearing the door right off its hinges. As upset as he could have been with my stupidity, he simply told me it was a mistake I needed to learn from and move past. His patience in that moment and in other moments like it has helped me take responsibility for my behavior, while never feeling that my destiny is somehow tied to something as stupid as backing out of the garage with the car door open.

"As a mentor, I see my dad as a lifelong learner and a genuine presence with those who have worked with him. I have had the chance to observe him in front of large audiences or speaking to one staff person in the hall outside of his office. It has always been apparent to me that the people who work with him know he cares about the details of their lives, their victories and defeats. They understand he is in a lifelong process of development and doesn't assume to have all the answers. When he recently visited one of my graduate classes, I was so moved when I noticed him taking notes on my lecture. After all his life lessons, he was still willing to learn from the ideas offered by his youngest son. I only hope others might see the same kind of genuineness in me that is so much a part of his leadership.

"Finally, my dad is one of my best friends. I recently had the opportunity to travel and work alongside him in Egypt. We had the time of our lives. Our work together was exciting, but didn't compare to the simple joy of getting to explore exotic parts of the world with someone you enjoy so much. At the conclusion of our travels in the Middle East, we watched the sun set on the shores of Tel Aviv and celebrated our trip together. I can't say any more than this: my dad is a whole lot of fun. I would travel the world with him anytime!"

The Best Bouquet

The story is told of a little fellow who asked for his pastor's boutonniere flower for his grandma as a love gift, and how the pastor, deeply touched, instead sent the big pulpit bouquet home to the grandma. The lad, his arms enfolding the bouquet, made one last statement: "What a wonderful day! I asked for one flower but got a beautiful bouquet." Now picture David McKenna surrounded by Janet, Doug, Debra, Suzanne, and Robert, and their spouses and children. What a bouquet!

POSTSCRIPT

If we work in marble, it will perish;
if on brass, time will efface it; if we rear up temples,
they will crumble into dust; but if we work
upon immortal minds and imbue them with principles,
with just fear of God and the love of our fellow men,
we engrave on those tablets something
that will brighten to all eternity.
—Daniel Webster